GO FISHING FOR
BREAM

GRAEME PULLEN

 The Oxford Illustrated Press

The Oxford Illustrated Press

© 1991, Graeme Pullen

ISBN 1 85509 223 9

Published by:
The Oxford Illustrated Press, Haynes Publishing Group, Sparkford, Nr Yeovil, Somerset BA22 7JJ, England.

Printed in England by:
J.H. Haynes & Co Limited, Sparkford, Nr Yeovil, Somerset.

A catalogue record for this book is available from the British Library.

Contents

Dedication

To my son Michael, who was born right in the middle of what would have been one of my Irish bream trips . . . I hope he carries my groundbait when he gets older!

Introduction

I well remember some years ago being fascinated by the British record fish list. As a youngster I could recite all the species in one go, but now I have difficulty remembering half of them. The species that drew my attention was the bream, and one of the old records stood at 13lb 8oz in 1945. It came from Chiddingstoke Lake, and the angler was a Mr. E. G. Costin. When I started to see photographs of really big bream in the angling press, I looked in awe upon those vast fish.

The bream is a laterally compressed fish. This means that when viewed from above it is narrow, but from a side-on view it takes on the lines of a dustbin lid. Since most anglers will never see a record bream, this book is devoted to all those people who just like catching them. They are not the world's most powerful fish, and the angler must scale down his tackle considerably to get the best sport from them. While the common bream attracts most anglers' attention, there is the added attraction of the silver bream, a separate species, or the hybrids, which are found largely in Irish waters and which have considerably more power than the common bream.

The size of fish you catch has nothing and everything to do with being an angler. All fishermen obviously want to catch the big fish, but some get a great deal more enjoyment from trying for the medium range fish of which there are more anyway, with the odd larger specimen as something to savour. Many articles and books have dwelt on the quest for record bream, but as an all-round angler for over thirty years, I can tell you that setting your sights a good deal lower than the British record will give you more enjoyment.

The size of common or bronze bream you are likely to encounter depends largely on the water you are fishing. Some of the newer gravel pits have already produced a growth potential that has seen the old British record of 13lb 8oz eclipsed many times. There are fewer fish in these specialist environments, but of those that are there, a higher proportion are likely to be in excess of 9lb. You will wait some time to record several big bream over this weight however, and on most waters the biggest fish will fall well short of that weight, simply because the environment in which the fish live is incapable of supporting such rapid growth. Bream are shoal fish, and a large shoal in a lake means that competition for the same food source levels out the weights. I would say 4lb is still a good size for a bronzie—and by that I mean a 4-lb fish that is properly weighed, with the weigh-sling deducted! Many anglers net bream and instantly call them four-pounders because the laterally compressed body makes them look big. I know, I've done it myself on occasions. You can look at a fish and say to yourself that it must surely be over 5lb, yet the spring balance asserts the truth, and 4lb is nearer the weight.

While some anglers regard bream as a bait-robbing pest, the majority enjoy catching them. To me, no fish should suffer derisory remarks or bad treatment. One day our mismanagement may well see their extinction, so it is in our own interests to protect all species in the water. Centuries ago bream were kept in stew ponds by the monks, and on Fridays bream and carp were put on the menu. Today, thankfully few people eat them and most are put back in the water to grow and provide pleasure for the next angler.

Should a large shoal of bream take up residence in front of you and decide to feed, then bream fishing will seem incredibly easy. There are times when they will take almost every conceivable bait you can throw at them, but at others they can drive you mad as they roll in front of you yet fail to dip the float or twitch the bite indicator. Such times are designed to set anglers thinking, and out of such frustrating days many new techniques and baits have been born. While it is possible to catch bream under most conditions, it is the angler who has the most knowledge and who fishes for them regularly who will score best. The bream is pretty basic, and is a creature of habit—it is up to you to find out his habits for the particular water you wish to fish. They can be found in lakes, gravel pits, canals, slow-flowing and on occasion rapid-flowing rivers. The behaviour and habits of bream will vary with the water it is living in. Bream in fast water need a different approach to those in the open waters of a large Irish lough. They are of course technically the same fish, but they will react so differently that you could be forgiven for thinking they are different species!

The other point about bream fishing is that you need to think big when it comes to the quantities of feed needed to attract them. A vast shoal of bronze bream will eat almost any amount of bait you throw at them. I once heard them called the 'swine of the lakes' in Ireland. Yet sometimes, when they just aren't in the mood for two buckets of feed, the crafty angler can still entice them to nibble a few morsels, even though they really don't

Several prebaiting sessions were needed to get these winter bream. Three anglers shared a catch of over 150lb from Yateley match pit, at the tail end of the season.

want anything at all. Feeding bream are easy to catch. Those that have no inclination to feed are not. But by careful choice of groundbaits, hookbaits and additives you may just be able to winkle a few fish out on a day when everyone else has written the water off as a waste of time. Maintaining good bream catches throughout a season is something of an art, and the best bream angler is something of a craftsman. Hopefully this book will put you on the path to success.

About The Fish

As I mentioned in the Introduction, there are two species of bream of interest to anglers—the bronze and the silver. There is also a hybrid, which in fighting terms is far better in my opinion than either of the other two. Up to the last decade or so many anglers thought the silver bream was in fact the young of the bronze bream, and things do become confusing when you realise that an immature bronze bream is silver in its younger stages! Now, however, research has established that there are two species. Both belong to the *Cyprinidae* family of coarse fish. The bronze or common bream has the Latin name of *Abramis brama* and the silver bream *Blicca bjoerkna*. They are the only species with a long anal fin to the rear of the belly, and that could be described as hump backed. The bronze bream is the larger of the two species, and is thought to have been recorded to $25\frac{1}{2}$lb in Finland. The British record fish reach into the lower double figures, so any angler wishing to top 15lb would be advised to try the warmer European waters. There the higher water temperatures, coupled with a more stable inland climate, must be more conducive to growing larger fish. Some European countries still kill coarse fish as food, however, and increased angling pressure must surely continue to limit the chances of any bream growing to 15lb or more without falling foul of an angler's bait.

Bronze Bream

The head of the bronze bream is best described as small, with the back humped in an arc and the tail fin deeply forked. Like the silver bream, they are laterally compressed, though not as much as the silver. Both species are covered with scales, but the bronze has an excessive covering of mucus which smears everything it comes into contact with—keepnets, landing nets, boots, jumpers and trousers, I've had them all coated liberally with bream slime on more than one occasion, and if you have never left a

About The Fish

The common or bronze bream at the top of the picture is markedly different from the immature or skimmer bream at the bottom. Note the sunken flesh at the rear of the bronze bream which means that it has spawned. The term 'skimmer' comes from match angling, because when the fish is hooked, it is small enough to be skimmed along the surface.

'breamy' keepnet inside your car on a hot summer's day, then you have missed an experience well worth missing! It can almost take the paint off the metalwork! Because of this liberal coating of mucus the bream has on occasions been mistreated by anglers fishing for other species. Yet the slime is there for a reason. It protects them from fungal infection, so perhaps they are more susceptible to disease than other species and the surplus of slime is their safety coating.

The colouring of this bream is basically drab. The back can be dark, even black, shading to a grey with a slight green sheen. The flanks are dark green to pale brown, and the belly is a dirty cream. They are a slow-moving species, as can be seen from the size of their fins, and they are quite tolerant of low oxygen levels. For this reason I believe that they may be the dominant species in many natural waters that are shallow, and in which the silt build-up has allowed a fringe of reeds to grow. Although reeds are pretty to look at, they do have the disadvantage of acting as a

9

trap for even more silt. Shallow lakes are prone to silting if they have an inflow stream affected directly by rainfall rather than aquifers. They silt up naturally as soil carried down the inflow in suspension reaches the main lake and settles. If the prevailing wind is south-westerly, the wave action will scour out the northern end of the lake, while the south remains shallow. The greatest growth of reeds will be in the shallow end, and of course increased reed growth can reduce the area of water available to fish. Shallow waters hold low oxygen levels in high summer, and I believe that this is why bream are the dominant species in many large, open, reed-fringed shallow waters. Of course angling clubs will have stocked their own favourite species and altered the natural ecological balance of the place. But in natural undisturbed waters, the bream should be the main species to fish for.

They spawn during the late spring and early summer, depending on the water temperature during this period. A cold spring may well prevent the water temperature from rising until early May, and spawning then runs into June or early July. As a general rule I have found that bream have spawned earlier than say tench. In Ireland, a country famous for its bream, the spawning may well be finished by mid-May, but then water temperatures could be higher there. The males are said to develop tubercles on their heads. I have caught a lot of fish with these tubercles, and I cannot understand why such a high proportion of my catches should have been males. Perhaps they had developed an appetite after spawning, but then surely the females would have been hungry as well.

It is also thought that they defend territories during spawning, but my opinion, having watched several groups in Ireland in clear shallow water, is that they are merely excited by the spawning activities of other bream. I have seen so many rolling through shallow weeds that I cannot support the theory that they pair.

This species lays yellow eggs of about 1.5mm in diameter. They stick to the fronds of the weeds growing in the shallows. The fact that water temperatures play an important part in spawning can be seen if you watch them carefully in May. They can be seen rolling in the slightly deeper water just out from the margins, and I feel sure that they are just waiting for the water in the shallows to reach a critical level. They can be spawning for a day or so, then if the weather changes there will be absolutely no ripples at all on the surface. A single ripe female may lay up to a quarter of a million eggs, but natural predation ensures that only a few survive into adult life; other coarse fish, and certainly eels, feed on this prolific lay of eggs. If there is extensive weed growth in the centre of the lake the bream will spawn there as well as in the margins, and again the water temperature will be the governing factor. Like all coarse fish bream are protected by a three-month close season from 15 March to 15 June.

About The Fish

That bream are a bottom feeding species, can be seen from their underslung mouths. The lips are extendable, allowing them to grub out food items on the bottom. They are cyprinids, with pharyngeal or throat teeth to help grind up the food they eat. For this reason they feed on the 'little and often' basis. All the angler has to do is get them into that feeding mood. As they are a shoal fish, competition for food is high, and once settled into an area they feed very confidently. Their food consists of planktonic crustacea, as well as midge larvae, otherwise known to anglers as bloodworm. Like tench and carp, they spend a good deal of their time rooting around soft mud, feeding on bloodworms. On a water with a soft mud bottom and a proliferation of bloodworms, you may well experience difficulty in weaning the bream off their natural diet, and onto your hookbait. I believe that bream are opportunist feeders and eat whatever they can, on the premise that if they don't, any one of a dozen or more cousins will eat it before them!

The distribution of the bronze bream is directly related to the availability of reed-fringed natural waters. Such low areas are not found up in the acidic mountain lakes, so Scotland and Wales have only limited numbers of the species. The lowlands of England and Ireland are well suited to bream, and the Cheshire meres, the Norfolk broads and the estate lakes of southern England are the best places to look. In Europe they are fairly common from the Pyrenees northwards to the Belgian and German borders. They will also tolerate brackish water and a few have been caught where a freshwater river enters the sea. Denmark has become popular recently for package trips by British anglers, and bream is high on the list of target species.

Silver Bream

The silver bream is less common than the bronze bream and it is something of a delicate creature. Because of its colour it can be mistaken for young bronze bream, but if anything it is even more laterally compressed. A silver bream that looks as though it should weigh over a 1lb will probably only pull the scales to 8 or 10oz. Silver bream used to be called white bream, presumably because of their lighter colour. Their colouring is altogether lighter than that of the bronze bream. They are grey-olive on the back and top of the head, lightening as you look down the flank into a silvery colour with a white underbelly. The fins are dark grey with a tinge of red or pink at the base. They are also very slimy, with an excessive covering of mucus, and have pronounced hump backs.

The average size, if there is such a thing, is from 6oz to 1lb. For some years the British record stood at just 1lb 8oz, so they are hardly a species worth spending too much time on.

11

Go Fishing for Bream

The best way to distinguish the silver from the bronze bream, especially with small fish, is by counting the rays on the fins. The silver bream has 3 unbranched and up to 23 branched rays on the anal fin, while the bronze bream has up to 28 branched rays. The dorsal fin has 8 branched rays, while that of the bronze bream has 9.

Silver bream dislike moving water and settle for heavily weeded waters, where they lay their yellow eggs during the months of May and June. Their appetite and diet is very much the same as the bronze, but obviously smaller and their distribution is also much the same. It has been said that they are only caught in the eastern half of the country, but with the netting and transfer of bronze bream by water authorities and angling clubs, the population of silver bream must also now be more widespread. The angler may find a few in the slower-moving canals, but they are a delicate fish and prefer a small, weedy lake, with plenty of food. Obviously, at only 1lb or so, they are unlikely to become a target species for the true bream enthusiast, but they may make an additional catch when out fishing for bronze bream. Where the two species co-exist, I believe that the gregarious nature of the bronze bream when feeding prevents the smaller silver bream from getting a look in. Silver bream are more likely to be caught on light float tackle in quieter water among lilies, rather than out in large expanses of open water.

Hybrids

Bream are not renowned for their fighting qualities, but if you scale down your tackle accordingly you can get some good sport from them. Perhaps the strongest bream is the hybrid. Larger than the silver bream, but smaller than the bronze, what they lack in size they make up for in tenacity. They have a jag-jag fight that is markedly different from any other fish, and on a float rod they are great fun. I probably enjoy taking 2-lb hybrids on a float rod more than a 4-lb bronze bream. As with so many species, the genetic crossing produces the strongest elements from both species. The two hybrids that are likely to be caught by the angler are crosses between the bronze bream and roach, and bronze bream and rudd. To the experienced eye they look different, and are identifiable, but to the untrained eye they are impossible to tell apart!

Ireland is particularly well known for its hybrid fishing, and such is the growth rate on some fish in areas like Carrickmacross in Co. Monaghan that I believe future anglers will travel there purely to experience the best hybrid fishing. Years ago there was concern when a roach of more than 3lb was reported, as this is the prime species for hybridising with the bream. A true roach of 3lb is still an incredible catch, but a hybrid of the same weight is barely worth reporting. It is also worth noting that

About The Fish

A 3-lb rudd/bream hybrid, a great scrapper for the match rod. A close-up of this hybrid reveals the unmistakeable extended lower jaw of a rudd.

cross-breeding occurs more often in still waters than in rivers in England. In Ireland however there are plenty of rivers where hybrids occur. I believe this is due to the fact that the larger loughs are linked by these rivers, which both bream and roach use for migration and spawning.

The spawning mediums used by roach, bream and to a certain extent rudd, are the same. Where areas of soft weed attract the female to lay their eggs, there is every chance of the milt from the males of any of the three species will cover those same eggs. I doubt whether they actually all spawn at the same time, but as they use the same areas, their eggs and milt obviously mix together. The hybrids are said to be sterile and therefore to pose no threat to the continuation of the 'pure' species, but anglers fishing Irish waters have assured me that they have caught second-generation hybrids, so there is some doubt about this. In cases like this I am more disposed to believe anglers than scientific officers, who often just take a random sampling. I don't doubt that many hybrids are sterile, but I think there are some that have bred naturally amongst themselves. The aquarist is familiar with genetically induced hybrids that have reproduced among themselves and produced an exact copy of themselves. I see no reason why this cannot happen in the wild. While aquarists can control conditions, there must be times when natural spawning conditions are ideal as well and breeding takes place.

If you catch a fish which displays even a few characteristics of roach or rudd, then it should immediately be regarded as a possible hybrid. Although there appear to be various inconsistencies in identifying hybrids, there are a few ways of assessing its parentage, such as examining the position of the fins, counting the number of rays in the fin, counting the number of scales along the lateral line and counting or noting the position of the pharyngeal or throat teeth. Scale counts along the lateral line were deemed to be a good way of differentiating between hybrids and true species, but the cross might not be genetically fifty/fifty. One hybrid may possess all the characteristics of the roach, while another may have more bream characteristics in it. Years ago I read a report by a roach specialist who referred to a fish known as a 'white roach' and another called a 'red roach'. They were not new species, merely a bream x roach hybrid and a bream x rudd hybrid respectively. So the problem of hybrid identification has been with us for scores of years. I have even heard that the microscopic examination of a scale from the lateral line of a hybrid revealed characteristics of both species, which is a scientific way of confirming the fish as a hybrid and not a true species.

This problem of identification is more important to the roach or rudd specialist than the bream angler as a hybrid is more likely to beat the existing British record for those species and therefore be disputed.

Hybrids are aggressive feeders and you can often be feeding a swim for bream, hit the odd fish or so, and find that a shoal of hybrids moves in. Even though they are smaller fish, their aggressive feeding habits push the bream out, especially when they intervene and take your bait before it has a chance to reach the bottom where you want it to lie for the bottom-feeding bronze bream. Because the hybrids are a cross with either roach or rudd, they have some of those species feeding instincts and will therefore feed either on the bottom or at mid water.

A rudd x bream hybrid will, if excited by regular feeding, take baits as soon as they hit the surface. If they are small, it can be infuriating when even with your shot placed only a foot from the bait, they grab it on the drop and prevent it from reaching the bream below. However, should the rudd x bream hybrids be larger, at 1½–2lb, they are worth catching on the float. Moving all your shot up under the float and shallowing the depth will bring them to net even faster. It all depends what you want, true bronze bream or the harder-scrapping but smaller hybrids.

In Ireland the record list includes hybrids, but in Britain they are not recognised for record listing. As a point of interest the Irish bream record is held with a fish of 11lb 2oz ironically caught by A. Pike! They have also recorded rudd x bream hybrids of 5lb 13½oz, and roach x bream hybrids of nearly 4lb, so you can understand the concern over hybrid identification among dedicated roach and rudd enthusiasts. The Irish specimen fish weight for roach x bream hybrids is 3lb, but only a few are recorded over that weight. The specimen weight for rudd x bream hybrids is also 3lb, but a good deal more are recorded by anglers. I class the rudd primarily as a stillwater fish, yet some of the Irish rudd x bream hybrids have been recorded from the River Shannon at Lanesborough and the River Liffey at Leixlip. I have no idea why this should be so. I would also have thought that as there are more roach in Irish waters, the percentage of roach hybridisation would be greater, but anglers report rudd x bream crosses as not only the larger but the more prolific hybrid. I can only think that there is more of an overlap in optimum breeding conditions in Irish waters between rudd and bream than between roach and bream. The only other theory I can suggest is that the rudd live in or near the prolific rush and weedbeds on the Irish waters. When the big bream shoals move in to spawn, their activity stimulates the rudd into spawning at the same time, so giving a greater influx of rudd x bream hybrids. This is pure speculation, but may be worth considering.

The hybrid is a good scrapper, and if the bream aren't about, I for one am not too disappointed when a shoal of 2- or 3-lb hybrids moves in. A good contact for a bream fisherman looking to put a specimen hybrid notch in his rod butt would be Norman Haworth. He specialises in fishing big bream and is currently engaged in trying to break the hybrid record from his base in Carrickmacross, Co. Monaghan. He runs an anglers' guest house and can be contacted at Roselinn Lodge, Carrickmacross, Co. Monaghan, Ireland. The two lakes near his home, Monalty and Naglack, have recorded more specimen Irish bream than any other venue. A trip there for hybrids could also result in some very good bream being caught!

Location

The rest of this book is concerned with the capture of bronze bream; the silver bream should be regarded as nothing more than a novelty catch. For the most part the bream angler should look for bronze bream in the larger open waters, that are shallow and possibly fringed with reeds. There will be few if any features in this type of venue, and you will have to rely solely on your ability to discover the likely feeding areas of bream. The most obvious way to do this is to ask other anglers or try your local tackle shop.

Large open waters are obviously susceptible to wind, and the constant ripple or wave action on the surface prevents visual location of the fish. However, the trained eye can often detect feeding fish by noting interference to the regular ripples being sent across the surface by the wind. In water of two feet or less a shoal of feeding bream will often disturb the surface. This throws up a 'flat' spot of water, almost like a miniature oil slick, which is caused by the bream tipping on its nose to root in the bottom, and its fanning tail fin disturbing the ripple action on the surface. On very windy days you won't be able to see this, but any surface disturbance should be noted and treated as a possible bream. If I spot such a disturbance when looking for new waters, I wait a minute or so in case it has been caused by a grebe, a diving duck or a coot. Then I catapult a big stone out to the side of the area. The impact of the stone often frightens the fish, and the arrowhead disturbance on the surface will indicate how large the shoal is. The best wind direction for spotting feeding fish in shallow water is southerly, or south-westerly; these winds are warm enough to increase water temperatures.

There may well be places on a featureless lake bed that the bream feed over more often. This would be a natural hot spot, perhaps owing to a proliferation of bloodworm in an area of soft mud. Subsurface weed growth would also act as a draw for shoaling bream. On flat, calm days the bream may be seen priming, or rolling through the surface. Bream experts can work out whether these rolling bream are likely to feed or whether they are simply getting ready for spawning. I can't tell, but I do know that fish priming like this on the surface after about July are very likely to be caught. Certainly any rolling bream should be treated as possible feeding fish, and the area at least noted down for a pre-baiting session.

Meres

Meres offer the angler classic shallow-water venues, and they invariably have a heavy covering of black silt. This silt has built up, perhaps over centuries, and is an ideal habitat for midges and gnats to breed in. Many

The large open lochs invariably have a shelf dropping away to a central plateau. By careful plumbing of the depth, and baiting up on the edge of the shelf, the angler can get good results. Here the author shows a catch of well over 100lb of bream.

meres are found towards the middle of England, and Cheshire, Shropshire and Staffordshire, all have their share.

One of my main concerns for the future is the changes in PH value that these northern waters might undergo. We have all heard of the problems of acid rain, which affects the hill and mountain lochs and reservoirs of Scotland and Wales, but I have never heard of the same changes taking place in the meres. Yet if the acid rain can kill off insect life in deep-water lochs, what will it do to the shallow meres, where the dilution rate is lower? It may well be that in the next twenty years acid rain, accelerated by global warming, will acidify the meres and the midges' and gnats' eggs will fail to hatch. This would mean a drastic reduction in the natural food supply of the bream, and while it might not lead to the decimation of stocks, it could result in a reduction in weight. Therefore the next five years might be the best time to try these shallow waters for big bream.

Having said that meres are shallow, I should perhaps point out that some are up to nine feet deep in the centre. Typically though, they are of even depth, with no sudden changes. They are alive with food in the summer months, when shrimps, snails and blooms of daphnia will all give the angler the impression that the bream are simply swimming around in soup! Some meres have a prolific weed growth, which helps the fish but not the fisherman. You should make sure that your swim is clear before putting a bait on the bottom. Meres are best fished from a boat, but it should be remembered that most are inaccessible because of the heavy growth of reeds and the generally boggy nature of the waterside margins.

Some meres are controlled by clubs or operated by a syndicate of limited membership. When this is the case, there should be some prepared swims running out to the water's edge and offering the angler a wide area of fishing. Three types of swim can be constructed. The Irish have many reed-fringed lakes, and they certainly have more than their fair share of boggy land. But they construct proper fishing platforms, with a narrow walkway out over the wet ground supported by either scaffold poles or wooden stakes. At the end of the walkway, which incidentally also has a hand-support rail, there is a T-head. This is the main platform, about five feet deep and fifteen feet long, allowing the anglers to fish at either end of the T-head, putting their bags and tackle boxes in the centre. A keepnet, should one be required, can be anchored to the corner. If properly constructed, these platforms can offer mere anglers access to parts of the water that may never have been fished before. They have a minimal effect on the wildlife or surrounding environment, as they blend in once the reeds have grown up around the edge of the platform and access walkway. During the close season and a couple of times during the summer, the rushes can be kept low by walking along the walkway with a strimmer. Done once, the cleared area should last for a couple of months.

Location

The second type of swim is constructed by boarding over four or five wooden pallets, floating them out to the edge of the rushes, using chest waders, then staking them into position. This prevents other anglers from capitalising on your hard work, as they too will need waders to reach the platform. This may be a selfish approach, but if one or two anglers go to the trouble of creating their own fishing area, then for the first week or so of the season at least, that swim should be treated as theirs. Alternatively, you might want to put some old empty oil drums (sealed up to prevent leakage) under the pallets to make a floating platform, that is lightly anchored. In that way you are free to move the whole platform if you want to try another area. A good way to drain an old oil drum, assuming it is already virtually empty, is to light a fire inside it. That will burn off any excess oil, and it can then be capped. Adult supervision is essential in this exercise. The floating platform is useful where either the water is more than a few inches deep or the ground is too soft to build the third type of swim.

The third type of swim involves carrying loads of hardcore out through the weeds and rushes—hence this is not practical if the ground is soft as it will all simply sink. You can build side supports out of railway sleepers topped by short scaffold poles. Finish off with a topping of clay to bind the surfaces of the hardcore and make some smaller tubes filled with earth to take the rod rests.

These are the three best bank platforms to fish from, but as I have said, ideally meres are best approached from a boat or punt, if the rules allow. Ideally, a punt, being oblong and flat bottomed, will make the better fishing platform, and if it is secured front and back, it is very stable. Keep the mooring ropes short, otherwise the punt will yaw slightly from end to end, and the bobbin indicators will rise and fall, giving false bite indications. By ramming poles into the lake bed and then mooring the punt at each corner, you can prevent any swinging at all. You may even want to leave the poles permanently in position for re-mooring at a future date.

The other advantage of using a boat is that you can always change swims to fish into any breeze. A strong wind is not conducive to good fishing or to the comfort of the angler, but as bream like to feed at the end of the lake where the wind is blowing, you have to put up with it. (The exception to this is a wind from an easterly direction, which not even the fish like.) Wind affects the position of food in a lake. In deep waters there are three layers of water temperature—a sort of stratification from surface to bottom. The thermocline is the central layer which is sandwiched between the epilimnion and the hypolimnion, and it tilts towards the end of the lake on to which the wind is blown. On a water which has no deep area, or which is no more than ten feet deep, this cannot happen, so I believe that daphnia and other surface-borne food items are carried along

19

by an undertow or current created by the wind and pulled to the down-wind end of the lake. As such a profusion of food will soon attract fish, this is why I always fish at the down wind end of any mere or lake.

A major problem with meres is that any early weed growth will die off quickly if there is a mild winter. According to the predictions of global warming, our winters may be getting milder, which in turn means an increase in weed growth as early as April. If we have a long dry spell by mid-June, that weed will have finished its growth cycle and then die off, with brown patches of algae and weed popping up to the surface. As the weed dies off, not only are oxygen levels reduced—which in turn puts the fish in a lethargic mood—but it creates problems with algal blooms in the water. When the water is very clear such algal blooms reproduce quickly, and a mere can soon turn the colour of pea soup. I have seldom had any luck fishing under such conditions, even though the blooms float only in the top few inches of surface water, while the water underneath is clear. The reason, I think, is that when this algal bloom dies off, it deoxygenates the water and makes the bream lethargic, despite their propensity for surviving with low oxygen levels.

In good conditions however, the many meres and broads still offer anglers fantastic potential for bags of medium-sized fish, and even record-weight bream. Many of these waters are still underfished by southern standards as there are fewer anglers about in these remote areas. Peace, tranquillity and a twitching bobbin is all that the bream angler requires.

Estate Lakes

While many estates are closed to anglers, there are still enough about to be worth mentioning. These venues are very similar to meres, except they will be different in shape and may have been constructed to be pleasing to the eye of the estate owner, with overhanging trees, bays, corners, inlets and outlets, and a wider variety of weed growth. The bottom will again be silty, probably from material washed down over the years from flooding on the inflow streams. A few will also have their own springs feeding them. There is the chance of a greater change in depth in estate waters, and it is often possible mentally to mark the likely areas without any other reference than a compass: the prevailing wind in Britain is south-westerly, so the wave action on the northern end of lakes will have eroded the silt and caused it to be deeper than the southerly end. If the water has an inflow stream, the chances are good that it will be near the shallower end of the lake, where floodwater has deposited silt. The exception to this rule is when the landscaper has constructed a silt trap to prevent unwanted suspended particles entering the lake. Only then will it be deeper.

The bream stocked in estate waters were probably put there either as

Location

Bream are a species that can be caught in almost any of our water systems. Estate lakes were often constructed to be pleasing to the eye of the estate owner, with bays, inlets, outlets, overhanging trees and a wider variety of weed growth.

ornamental fish along with carp and tench, or as a stocking from another water by a controlling club. Either way, shoals of bream soon adapted to the soft mud bottom, though there seems to be something lacking in the water, which prevents them from achieving exceptional weights. I can only guess why this is. Possibly it's the lack of freshwater shrimp which give better growth rates than other foods, or because bream tend to overbreed in the confines of the estate lake. Through overbreeding they become stunted, and while some anglers might like popping out bream after bream under 2lb, the serious angler will always prefer the satisfying thump as his rod hits into a fish of 4lb or more.

A natural stocking of bream over a period of years, provided they have not been interfered with through netting and restocking, will grow as a shoal at a set rate. A few may increase by a few ounces over their brothers, probably through being more competitive when feeding, but the difference

21

will be minimal. It is when a shoal reduces in numbers—from poor bankside handling or from stress through cold winters or the rigours of spawning for example—that the competition for food is reduced, and those that remain grow larger faster. The ultimate goal as far as the specimen hunter is concerned is to find an estate lake holding just one shoal of bream that has had a gradual reduction in numbers over the years. In that shoal there will be three or four leviathans, and those are the fish you will be aiming for.

There could be another factor inhibiting an estate lake's development into a good bream water. Estates will invariably be largely self-supporting, in that they will have enormous expanses around them given over to farming. The feeder stream that fills the lake will probably run through this farmland, and if the estate is in southern or eastern England, there will almost certainly be a run-off of fertilisers into the stream and so into the estate lake. These fertilisers cause havoc in the reproductive cycles of all freshwater species, including bream. When a dry spell extends for several months, the chemicals remain on the ground. In heavy rainstorms, they are then flushed into the lake, where they inhibit spawning fish, egg hatch and fry survival rates, and contaminate the entire ecosystem. Nitrate run-off will cause weed and algal blooms, the dying weed in turn deoxygenating water. While bream are capable of surviving low oxygen levels, low levels don't enhance their growth rates or reproductive qualities. The future of estate waters lies in the balance, and I think that some may be totally upset by stockings of various other species of fish.

Estate waters pose the same problems of shoal location as meres, but as many of them are surrounded by trees, there will be slick-calm areas in the summer that offer the angler a chance to locate surface-rolling fish, particularly with binoculars. A good deal of time should be devoted to locating the bream. In an estate water they will have two or three defined feeding areas, probably two in the summer and autumn and a third, different one in the winter. It is up to you to find these spots. While mere fish have regular patrolling routes and can be caught by placing food in one of them, the estate fish have no defined patrol, and can move into the feeding area from any direction of the compass. Doubtless they can be caught by pure chance if your bait is in their path, but for the most part you should concentrate the feed in the one or two areas where you have seen activity. By taking note of rolling or finning bream you see through your binoculars, you can at least do some pre-baiting in the knowledge that at some period the bream are in that spot. If you catch a few there, stick at it, but if you only pick up one fish, watch again and bait another area where you see the fish moving.

There is one exception to this approach, and that is directly after the season has started, following a cold spring. The bream may be running late with their spawning, and the surface activity you see will then be connected with this process. It will occur in shallow water, near weedbeds or right in the margins. No amount of pre-baiting will put them off spawning, and the amateur may waste both bait and fishing time at these spots. The activity you want is in deeper water, possibly some way out, which you can see easily in a glassy calm.

Once I have decided that the bream are in one of their summer or autumn feeding areas I put in a lot of bait over a period of about three days, and providing weather conditions are favourable I would be disappointed not to take quite a few fish. In winter the shoal of bream will be tighter and they will tend to stay in one small area. Contrary to popular opinion they can still be caught, even in the depths of winter. Their winter feeding area may be more difficult to find, and it is generally in a totally different spot to the summer and autumn areas. Visual location is almost impossible, as winter weather is blustery and wet when it is mild, and if it is still and calm the lake simply freezes over! Therefore I suggest that you plumb the entire lake looking for a deep hole near some bankside trees if possible. Most estate waters have some trees around the edges, and if the deep water is in this vicinity you have a spot worth trying.

I assume that the bream shoal up in the deeper water because the temperature may be more stable there when a cold snap occurs. I also think that they become lethargic during such conditions and rarely move elsewhere to feed. Like many species they must live off stored body fats accumulated through the rich feeding of the summer months. They can be caught, but you must first feed the swim very lightly, and with a slow sinking cloud groundbait, perhaps with added oils. The local tackle shop will be able to advise you on the brand used by most matchmen. The bream will probably be hanging around a third of the way off the bottom, occasionally finning and cruising slowly. Heavy balls of groundbait will destroy any chances of fish, and you must tickle their appetites by fishing light, with perhaps a single pinkie for hookbait and an occasional small ball of cloudbait. You want the groundbait to tumble through the water layers slowly, and follow up with the odd feed of pinkies or red maggots as loose feed.

I doubt very much whether you'll catch a huge bag of bream at first, but even only two or three will at least confirm you are in the right place. Casters make an excellent bait in the colder months, and adding them to the cloudbait, especially if the caster is dark brown, will make it sink slower. Bites can be pretty delicate, so be prepared to watch the float or quivertip very carefully indeed.

As an illustration of just how fickle winter bream can be I have to recount a session undertaken by Nigel Newport from my local tackle shop. Nigel had been fishing the North Lake at the Yateley Leisure Sport

Go Fishing for Bream

Nigel Newport unhooks a bream from Yateley's match pit—part of a 90-lb-plus haul he took in the winter. He is using a plastic disgorger to extract the hook, but artery forceps are handy when worm fishing, as bream occasionally take this bait deep.

Complex for bream that he knew were there somewhere. Although he had adopted the 'light' approach to feeding, he just couldn't touch a fish. He decided to wait until a mild spell, with the air temperature rising fast, and threw a large summer dose of feed into a swim. He left it for a couple of days, but by that time the weather had turned cold again. After fishing the swim for a couple of hours he was about to go home totally biteless when he spotted a half caster casing hanging on the bend of his hook.

Although he had used casters in the pre-bait mix he had used none in the feed he was fishing with. A sucked caster case meant that there were fish out there feeding, probably tentatively, but at least they were there. A tiny detail like that would in all probability be missed by many anglers, but it was noticing and interpreting this that enabled him to fish on with confidence. When Nigel realised they were not getting their heads down

24

and demolishing the feed, he resorted to a size 22, single red maggot and a small feeder lightly packed with damp brown groundbait. Rather than leave the feeder in one spot, he twitched it back over the bottom every couple of minutes until he got a bite. By fishing on into the late afternoon he started to fill his net, until just before dark his bag of bream weighed 91lb 2oz. Although they weren't large fish—they ranged in size from 2lb to 4lb, nevertheless, they were great sport for the depths of winter.

About a month later, just before the close of the 1989 season I was at the Yateley Leisure Sport Complex where the conditions are similar to an estate lake, just before dusk, pre-baiting an area with Nigel for a last-ditch session he was having with some friends. They were there to fish one of the main carp pits, but had located a vast shoal of bream near an island. The water was of medium depth, around six to eight feet, and the shoal was resting about twenty yards out. As the winds made long-distance float fishing impossible, they chose to use a light swimfeeder rig in conjunction with a quivertip. As the bites would be gentle, they opted to use a target board to help see the bites better. We filled in the swims with a slow-sink groundbait and maggots over about three days.

On the day scheduled for fishing I was called away on a job and I arrived at the lakes with just half an hour of usable light left. One of the party who was fishing the opposite bank and casting across into the same swim had some bream in the net, but had also caught superb roach to 1lb 7oz and a cracking winter tench of 6lb 12oz—not bad on the last day of the season! The other lads had bream to just over 4lb, while Nigel took over 95lb, with bream to nearly 5lb, and some roach to 1lb 14oz. In total the group had over 170lb of fish, primarily bream, taken at a time of year when many people would have been sitting at home.

So you can see that bream fishing offers a chance of success to anyone who is prepared to put in a little time and a great deal of effort. In the summer this same shoal of bream will doubtless go elsewhere. I have heard it said that bream travel on their patrol routes because they are territorial. I cannot agree with this as I interpret 'territorial' as meaning to guard against others who might move into your area. Bream are surely the least aggressive fish in the water, and in any case, what other species would they be warding off? I think that when patrolling, they are just moving between feeding areas. On a mere this can be some distance, while on a smaller estate water, the feeding areas are closer together.

For some reason, clear waters encourage fish to grow big, but they are always difficult to catch. I presume that they grow big because the stronger light penetration allows prolific weed growth, which in turn supports high protein feed in the shape of freshwater shrimp. But the fact that the bigger bream become difficult to catch I can only attribute to the clearer water making them naturally more nervous about potential predation, though this doesn't explain why they're still difficult to catch at night, when they can't see anything.

Gravel Pits

This is where the bulk of the big bream come from. A newly excavated, and then flooded, gravel pit affords superb opportunities for pushing fish growth rates up fast. Of course bream need to be stocked as small fish as soon as possible after the lake has filled—generally about a year is reckoned to be sufficient for the aquatic life-cycle to get underway. Many of the southern gravel pits came about through the building of motorways, which require gravel in the construction. Hence some venues have multi-

Fishing the pole for bream at a Hampshire gravel pit. If the fish are moving close to your bank and the water is coloured, you can take bream on light tackle when traditional tactics fail.

water complexes very close together, and fish stocks can be similar in all of them. One of the most famous waters for big bream is known as the T.C. pit near Oxford. Gravel from here was used in the construction of the A34 ring road but it is now possibly the most famous big bream water in the British Isles. It is hard to fish, but it eventually produced low double-figure fish, and subsequently even larger fish.

On the face of it, trying to locate bream in a gravel pit seems difficult because they are invariably deep. Gravel is seldom found over a wide area and to a uniform depth, and the variation in the depth of water reflects this. The water is shallow where the gravel was thinnest and deep where it was more readily available. The extraction companies also use a technique called 'throwback', which means that the contours on the bottom rise and fall sharply, creating gravel shallows or bars and deeper channels called dropoffs. If the pit has been excavated with the 'throwback' technique, you will have a good chance of finding the bream in one of the deep channels.

Bream will seldom come right up on top of a 12-inch deep gravel bar, except perhaps to spawn, but in summer they certainly feed along the edges of the deep water. If the gravel pit you intend fishing is heavily fished I suggest you start by spending some time making your own map and plumbing the depth all over the lake. You need a good working knowledge of the bottom contour, and plumbing, combined with chats with the local water bailiff should give you a good basis to start on. Hard-fished waters will see the main bream shoal in the deepest channel out towards the centre of the pit. They will have learned to associate anglers' lines with being caught, and the deeper water gives them the confidence they need. A great many carp waters are now stocked with big carp and are heavily fished. At the time of writing, the vogue is for bolt-rigs and self-hooking techniques that mean the line is tight from lead to rod top. The bream don't like these tight lines (nor do carp for that matter), and bailiffs have told me that the fish often refuse to cross an imaginary boundary, marked by an angler's tight line. During daytime in the summer, and also during the winter, your best bet is to stick to the largest main channel between gravel bars that you can find.

During darkness however, the bream will often move into other channels to feed, but again you should bait up on the slope of the channel rather than down in the pit. One problem that does arise from a particularly sharp drop on a channel edge is that the mainline will be lying across it. You can overcome this by moving swims until you are casting directly up the channel rather than approaching it from the side. That way your line is lying along the bottom evenly, and in addition to avoiding a break-off on the strike, you get a much better bite. Bits of twigs, debris and weed will have lodged on the tops of the gravel bars, so if your cast is over the edge you may have a problem or two. Of course there may not be a swim access to allow you to cast directly down the mouth of the channel, and you then have to make the best of a bad job.

Assuming that you have located your bream and you cast into the channel, make sure the rig is lying on the edge of the gravel bar nearest to you. If you cast to the opposite slope of the channel you will have a tight line suspended off the bottom over the central main channel. To the bream this looks no different from the self-hooking carp rigs, and the chances are that they won't go near the hookbait. The mainline of a bream angler is perhaps 4lb, while a carp angler may have 8–12lb, but I don't think it is the diameter that frightens the fish, but the fact that the line is tight. If you are fishing with a quivertip the line will still be relatively tight from rod top to feeder, but if you fish with your rod at a lower angle, the line will be along the bottom where fish are less likely to bump into it.

It is worth noting that carp anglers actually do a lot to feed the bream. On big unfished open waters like the Irish loughs, you have to supplement the pre-baiting with—more pre-baiting! There is simply not enough bait going into the Irish waters to get the bream educated. Bream fishing has always had a reputation for using huge portions of groundbait, and rightly so. A big shoal can eat a considerable amount of groundbait. Carp fishermen help by distributing large quantities of boilies in the water which also happen to be a favourite of bream. Bearing in mind the expense of a heavy pre-baiting session with shop-bought boilies, it is little wonder the carp fisherman doesn't take too kindly to a shoal of bream moving in on them, but still it pays the bream angler who is looking at a gravel pit heavily fished for carp to see what system the carp anglers are using.

A great many carp anglers pre-bait using mini-boilies to get the carp interested in their hookbait, and then fish one or two boilies over a bed of the mini-boilies. If that is the technique being used, the bream will be scooping up the mini-boilies with glee. All the bream angler has to do is fish the same swim as the carp angler, using a swimfeeder rig terminating in a mini-boilie on the hook. This could lead to two problems, however. Firstly, it will become apparent that you can't get to many of the 'live-in' carp swims until the colder weather arrives in September. Secondly, you will find you have a better than even chance of catching a big carp! This is not very good for your rod, and even less so for your relations with the carp angler who sees you net a twenty-pounder! That's fishing though, and I strongly advise you to adapt to fishing mini-boilies when you know that they are being introduced to the water in large quantities.

Many of the pits featuring 'throwback' topography also offer some deeper channels, although on a smaller scale, close to the bank. I see little need for legering close in such a situation, except perhaps in bright sunlight when floatfishing would be a pleasant alternative. While I have taken some reasonable nets of bream over the years, the vast majority have fallen to leger rigs. Perhaps because I don't get the chance to do it quite so often I like the prospect of floatfishing. Find a quiet corner, bait it up over a couple of days and you will often be pleasantly surprised as to the outcome. I have not yet hit the 100-lb target on the float, but it is a prospect I look forward to.

Some bream anglers dislike fishing pits with a varied bottom as they can't decide which particular gully they should be fishing. If you adapt yourself to suit the pit you can often place a bait in either one of two gullies and so keep your options open as to shoal location. This happened to me once at Pit 5 in the Hollybush Lane complex at Farnborough. I wasn't after bream in particular, just fish of any description, and I turned up never having seen or fished the pit before. It was 15 June and naturally all the better swims were occupied. I walked over to the bailiff who sent me down to the farthest end of the pit and as I walked away I'm sure I heard him giggling with his other friends.

I set up opposite an island and could see from the outlying topography that a continuation of the island spit probably ran straight towards me. That would give deeper areas either side of the bar. Plumbing with a float confirmed this, and I baited with sweetcorn—just one tinful—in both channels. I got no sleep that night. In the morning the bailiff came round as I was playing out another tench. His friends were with him. They seemed a little surprised to see a bent rod, and even more surprised to see a throbbing keepnet in the water. I thanked him graciously for the superb information he had given me about the swim, and I could see from his red face that he felt pretty foolish. Before asking them to assist with my photography I asked him how he had fared but he had caught only two tench. My net weighed 118lb 7oz if I recall correctly, and to my amazement I even managed to get the same swim two nights later. I baited either side of the bar again, and by morning my net contained bream, tench and one carp to a weight of 124lb.

I took another angler there at the end of the week and we had a 'poor' session with 80lb between us, including a 21-lb pike hooked fairly in the scissors, at night, with only a single grain of sweetcorn as bait. I still don't believe that pike took the corn. I had seen Paul's bobbin go up in confident fashion, and the initial strike was the bump-bump of a bream. Then it went solid, and in the pitch black we netted what I thought was one of the pit's big carp. Imagine our surprise when the torchlight revealed a huge pike! Such are the success stories of fishing double channels at pits.

While a good area to try for pit bream is in the deep water either side of a spit of land jutting out into the main body of water, my preference is for fishing directly off the end of the spit. On larger pits particularly, I believe that bream patrol regularly, and if they run into a bay and follow the contour around, they obviously have to pass by the end of the spit. They may not stop to feed under normal circumstances in such a place, but it does at least make a good point for placing your bait. Of course you don't know the fish are resident there, so you can't fish the area with confidence—in that respect it is something of a gamble. But it does mean you can lay a baited patch down, knowing that at some time the shoal of bream will pass by. This principle is often applied by specimen bream anglers after double-figure fish. They bait a pitch up on the premise that sooner or later a shoal of very big fish will pass by. My argument is that there are parts of a gravel pit—indeed of any water—that the fish never go to. At least by fishing the interception approach there is a good chance that they will pass over your baited patch—whether they take your bait or not though is what keeps us all going back again and again!

A point worth noting with gravel pits is that if they are reasonably well established, there might be two or three generations of bream in there, and they are likely to be of different weights, the oldest being the heaviest. I also believe that the different generations shoal separately and have differ-ent patrol routes. I have never, for instance, caught a 1-lb skimmer, a five-pounder and a seven-pounder in the same session. I believe that within a pound or so, the first fish you hook is a fairly good indication of the size range to expect.

Another tip is to look to the fringe of weedbeds as a location that might attract bream. Bream are more delicate feeders than tench or carp and so are unlikely to bury their heads deep into thick weed and be found in the middle. And although I have long held the view that if you raked and baited a weedbed enough you would be able to catch any species there, in my experience bream don't respond half as well as say, carp or tench. Why this should be I don't know, but bream just haven't come to my net from such clearing operations and I have heard the same story from other anglers.

What bream do respond to, is a minimum of dragging on the edge of a main weedbed, and I believe that this is because they are creatures of habit. Extensive dragging of an area they know well from their patrolling routes must alarm them, and they may very possibly actually shy away from such a place until they accept the new features. The only time I believe it could be done is that critical time when the bream are away from their patrolling routes and engrossed in spawning. If you clear the area well while they are away it should be accepted by them more quickly when they return.

Gravel pits offer a wide range of techniques, baits, problems and topography, and different-sized bream. Whether you want to sit for days (and nights) after just one huge bream, whether you want 100lb of fish to 5lb, or whether you want skimmer bream on the pole, gravel pits will provide the fishing for you.

Canals

I have never been a great lover of canals, even though I have lived no more than a mile from the famous old Basingstoke Canal for nearly forty years. I cannot see a large catch of any species ever being caught from such a long, narrow stretch of water. I also think that if you do get a shoal of fish in front of you, and hook one, the rest will become spooked in such a confined space. Having said that however, I have to acknowledge that some canals do indeed produce big bags of fish.

As far as I know canals have never held bream into double figures and this is despite the fact that the canals are rich in feed and are technically suitable for supporting such fish. Possible reasons are the bankside activity which may be greater on a canal, and the boat traffic. Of course, there are plenty of bream and boats on places like the Norfolk Broads or the River Shannon in Ireland, but both these places offer areas of escape for

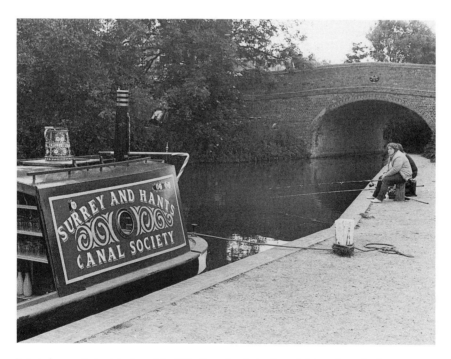

Bream in canals tend to be a bit difficult and pole tactics might produce the better sport. Early and late in the day are the best times to fish, when boat traffic is at a minimum.

spooked fish—the Broads are expansive and the River Shannon is forty yards wide in places—whereas the narrowness of the canals makes it more difficult for the fish to escape. The Irish canals with little boat traffic would afford the best chance of a good fish, but even there, bream are unlikely to top 4lb—a 5- or 6-lb specimen would be an excellent fish.

While bream run lengths of the canal in their patrolling routes, it is the old cuts and the flashes which were used for turning the barges around that draw me the most. You can, of course, bait up in the middle of a canal virtually anywhere along its length and fish the interception technique I suggested in the gravel pit section, but I would think that unless Lady Luck is on your side you could have a substantial wait. Better to bait up in one of these wider turning areas, as they are less likely to be used nowadays and I have found that the fish stay there for some length of time, particularly during cold winter weather.

You can leger for them, as most anglers do, but I find that the waggler float comes into its own here. You often have little distance to cast, and the surface is relatively calm. Some canals have a little flow on them, particularly after heavy rain. If you fish the main channel this can cause the waggler to sink slowly under the surface, and if the bait is dragging bottom you then get a false bite. While this may not be so apparent when floatfishing the flash or turning area, I would suggest dispensing with a float in these areas and using a swingtip instead. A quivertip with a very light tip could be used, but I feel that there would not be sufficient 'draw' on the current to warrant its use. You still need as delicate a bite indication as you can get and the swingtip will still allow this, while being heavy enough to counteract any drag.

Some canals will have been dredged to maintain access for boat users, and if they are then stocked by angling clubs they should provide a viable venue for the bream angler. Such a canal will have a central deep channel, kept clear by the action of the boat's propeller's. This is the place to bait up, right in the centre of the canal, where the bream should be patrolling. They can travel some distance up and down a length of canal, and will generally have a turning point near a curve where a weedbed may be a bit thicker. This marks the end of their route, and after reaching it they patrol back to the other end again. In high summer it is easy to see this weedbed, but in coloured water you will have to fish on a trial-and-error basis.

While all canals have a towpath on which the horses used to pull the barges, the bank opposite the towpath can be overgrown. There may be a single overhanging tree or even a row of bushes. Whatever bankside vegetation hangs over the canal, you should treat it as a possible bream-holding feature. The bream will not continually run up and down a set length of canal. As evening draws in, and boat and bankside activity ceases, they too will slow up and often return for the night to stay near this feature. By baiting up near here you should pick fish up as light fades in the evening. The beauty of bream fishing on a canal is not so much the size or numbers of fish you are likely to catch, but the tranquillity and beauty of your surroundings.

Slow-Moving Rivers

While many anglers claim that the best bream fishing comes from a stillwater, you should never discount slow-moving rivers. They can range from a river as large as the Thames in summer flow conditions to the mighty Shannon in Ireland—surely the greatest bream river of all. The heaviest bags ever recorded by anglers, both individual or group, may have come from stillwaters, but some truly incredible bags have come from slow-moving rivers.

Providing I know that a stretch has some bream in it, I have great confidence in fishing over a baited patch on these slow rivers. I believe the activities of fry feeding over a baited patch in the initial stages attract bream from downstream. There must also be some particles of your groundbait mix that sink more slowly and therefore end up further

Nigel Newport with a super bag of bream, hybrids and skimmers, plus some roach, taken from a slow-moving river using the pole.

A Thames bream slides towards the waiting net of this angler. Once on their side, constant pressure will ease the fish up on the surface where you should have no trouble netting it.

downstream, which will also possibly draw a shoal up towards you. In a stillwater that groundbait goes straight down, but in a river it can stretch downstream in a line. If your groundbaiting is accurate that line should be narrow, so any shoal running up it has a better chance of reaching your hookbait. This is where the term 'fishing a line', comes from and it applies to floatfishing as well as to the leger.

The bream shoals migrate in the large rivers, sometimes on a regular patrol route, sometimes due to spawning. Where they get this urge to run the river like salmon I have no idea, but if there are locks and weirs on the river, the bream will often run up into the fast water to clean themselves off after spawning. The best time to take them is when they are running upstream, as I believe that they are then hungry from the rigours of spawning and consequently feed better. When they have cleaned off in the fast water and are dropping back downstream to settle into a normal life again, they can still be caught, but they don't seem to feed quite so ravenously.

Once they start to feel the cooler water coming with the advent of autumn, they settle into shorter patrolling lengths, and like the canal bream, they will set up station near some sort of feature. On the Shannon and the Thames, for instance, islands are a good feature. You would think they would lie at the tail of the island, keeping downstream where the flow is better, yet I have had my better catches in the autumn by fishing on the upstream end of an island, and slightly to one side. I believe that any food items coming downstream are diverted across from the front of the island and concentrate into a tighter flow area down the side. Therefore the fish has less work to do if it wants to pick up current-borne offerings. Certainly chub on these slow rivers will stay tight up against any overhang of bushes or trees, and they are there, I believe, for the very same reason. Such an area can only really be fished efficiently with a leger rod. On the smaller rivers floatfishing with a bodied Avon float can be fun, and allows you to pick up the main shoal's position as you can run the float down the entire length of baited patch until you hit a fish. The larger rivers require heavy-bodied wagglers, but apart from the difficulty of mending the line when waggler fishing, you will always get some sort of wind over the water. Waggler fishing needs an even-paced current to prevent the line bellying out and dragging the float under, giving a false bite. An island will divert the current flow enough to make the float difficult to control, so if you do fish a waggler, try to do so on an open, featureless spot.

The bream's preference for islands was illustrated to me on a trip to the Thames. Word had come into my local tackle shop that a large shoal of bream might be taking up residence near some islands above Reading. The manager, Nigel Newport, had the first hit, then I went down with him to write a feature on the trip. Would the bream stay there? We fished from the same swim and Nigel fished one quivertip rod while I fished two. We concentrated on feeding a line about 6ft out from the front side of an island, and only picked up a few perch. We put in more caster-laced groundbait, and eventually picked the odd bream up on red maggots. I'm a great believer in worms, especially small brandlings, and used a cocktail of worms, tipping off with maggots to get the bigger fish.

The first bream came to my downstream rod and I followed it with a couple more. That told me that the main shoal was still down below us, so we put in more feed to pull them up. I then started to get line bites on the downstream rod, but hooked fish on the upstream one. This indicated that the shoal was moving up. Nigel picked up more fish so in went more groundbait. By midday we thought we had passed the magic 'ton', then in the afternoon bites tailed off. We put in more feed, then relaxed until more bites came in the late afternoon, when boating activity dropped off. I often wonder whether the boats bother the anglers more than they bother the fish. I certainly didn't appreciate the 'flat-out' brigade who sent a wave of water slapping up the bank. But then sometimes the rhythmic nodding of the quivertip continued while the boats were passing! The bream were back. We packed up in order to weigh in with enough light for photographs, and we were both delighted to tot up the weights on a great bream catch. We weighed in at a little over 202lb! The average fish was typical for the Thames—$2\frac{3}{4}$–$3\frac{1}{4}$lb—but we had a few at 4 and 5lb. The shoal stayed by that island right into November, until the cold weather screwed everything down and winter floods presumably moved it to deeper water.

Islands represent the best features you are ever going to find on a slow-moving river, but there are others. In small rivers there will always be bends, and these bends are deep on the outside where winter floods have ferried the silt away and shallow on the inside. Bream shoals often rest at the downstream, inside edge of one of these bends, presumably for ease of feeding on free-flowing food items. When grubbing about on the bottom, they presumably move further up the inside of the bend, as this is where the silt deposit will be greatest, and therefore where the weed and insect life is thickest. On a small river, especially on a bend, you can use a bodied Avon float, and still mend the line to prevent any slack, without disturbing the flow of the float.

Place your bait on the upstream end of the swim and, feeding at regular intervals, send the float right through the bend to the downstream end. The chances are good of getting a bite towards the tail of the bend, but if the bream are at all inclined to feed they will move right upstream, virtually on top of the baited patch. The float should be set to trip the bait right along the bottom, as bream in a river seldom rise too high to take a bait. You should also vary the line your float takes through the bend. When the groundbait goes down it is heavy enough in a ball to sink straight to the bottom. But any loose feed might be whisked away by the current at a different angle and take the feeding bream with it. Therefore you should try 2ft both inside and outside from your direct line of feed. Most anglers concentrate on a central feed line for too long.

In Ireland you have many rivers to choose from and here you'll need plenty of groundbait. Many are tributaries of the mighty River Shannon, and yet all produce big single specimens and monster bags of fish. While there will be bream shoals at various venues along its length, any Irish river will by English standards, be grossly underfished. I would therefore suggest that you confine your slow-river breaming in Ireland to venues that have been tried and tested over the years. The Irish Tourist Board will be able to supply you with a list of guest-house accommodation along the lengths of the Shannon where bream fishing is popular, and the guest-house owners will be more than delighted to tell you which stretches to fish. Bait can be booked in advance, and at the better guest houses, the owners will even go out and pre-bait a stretch of river for your arrival! They work on the theory that if you catch bream while staying at the guest house you are very likely to return the following year and recommend them to your friends. Ireland is my favourite place for freshwater fishing as pressure by anglers on English waters reaches breaking point, and I love the quiet solitude of a complete lake or river to myself. However, when breaming, I like to fish where there are other anglers, as feed will have been going in on a regular basis and the fish will not need educating to my hookbaits. One of the problems with fishing a little-known venue is that it may be full of fish, but they may never have seen an angler's bait before, and therefore be difficult to wean off their natural diet. I simply haven't the time to spend three days pre-baiting a river to get the bream on to my feed. I would sooner risk competition from other anglers on swims, knowing that if I get there, the fish should come straight on the feed.

While on a fishing holiday in Ireland, I have noticed that while English anglers get up at the crack of dawn to grab a swim at home, they fish at a more leisurely pace on holiday. Guest-house breakfasts are normally enormous affairs in Ireland, and with a night on the Guinness or Smithwicks the night before, many don't leave their accommodation until 10am. I can get up at dawn, fish till 9am, then while a friend watches the swim, nip back for a hearty breakfast and swap places when I return. We get the best swim, extra fishing time and still have the enormous Irish breakfast—not a bad system!

Fast Waters

Having said that the bream is a lover of still or sluggish water, we have to acknowledge that some bream can be found in fast waters. Most species of coarse fish can survive under a number of unconducive conditions. It is survival of the fittest I suppose, and fast-water bream certainly are fighters. Their broad flanks put up considerable resistance to a current, so they dive and plunge rather like a chub. Living in, and fighting the current tones their muscles up.

The first time I came into contact with fast-water bream was on the Royalty Fishery of the Hampshire Avon. I was fishing the upstream end of the piles at the railway swim, and had a run of deep water in front of me, where I could see—barbel, chub, and roach—but slightly upstream it was scoured out and I couldn't quite make out the shapes in that area. It was a bright sunny summer day and the barbel were not responding so I heaped in feed farther upstream than normal, and left the swim to look for some chub. When I returned the area was black with fish and I could see they were the fish I'd previously seen further upstream. I tried bunches of maggots, I legered on the bottom with a feeder and maggots, and finally tried a single grain of sweetcorn. Suddenly I saw a bream turn round to swim downstream and take it.

After that I put about a tinful of corn in the swim using a baitdropper, and stood watching the bream graze over the bottom. As I ran the float through, they obviously saw the line and shot in the clear water, and *en masse*, turned round, disappeared downriver and slowly returned when the float had gone through. I couldn't imagine that they were so spooky as to realise that the extraction of one of their number spelt danger, but I couldn't catch them. They were feeding, because when they started in at the tail of the swim, the lead fish would tilt on his nose and pick off the grains of corn, working up towards the main baited area. The rest of the shoal, consisting of twelve to fifteen fish followed. My problem was that I was casting upstream then retrieving as the float came down the swim towards me. There was obviously a bow in the line from the current, and I couldn't hold the float back to make the hookbait precede the line and shot. I took off the float, slid two bb shot about a foot from the hook, cast out and as soon as the bait started towards me kept pace with the current by winding and holding the match rod high to keep excess line off the surface. This satisfied the bream more, and I struck when I saw the bow in the line twitch. I missed a great many, which I assume were line bites.

The art in fishing fast waters appears to be to dispense with maggots, which draws too many bites from unwanted roach or dace. Use a particle bait like sweetcorn or tares that sink fairly quickly and gets down to the bottom. The hook size need be no larger than 10—gilt if you are on corn—and use just 3-lb line straight through. A match rod is ideal for controlling the tackle, and closed-face reels are adequate for this size of fish. Doubtless a shoal of bream will come on to a heavy baiting in a swim, and perhaps you will have to lay down a carpet of groundbait to get them interested. But what appears to put them off is the introduction of heavy balls of groundbait once they have their heads down over the feed. In stillwater the opposite appears to be true, and once fully engrossed with feeding, stillwater bream will rarely move until they have eaten everything. It is better to get them browsing through the swim on groundbait, then get them actually feeding by introducing particles like sweetcorn. If you must leger—and I favour the float or freeline for these river fish—use a large piece of flake for hookbait. Barbel and chub might hammer an Avon rod round when they bite, but bream give a delicate tweak. I advise using an Avon quivertip rod like the Ryobi model.

Just how hard river bream can feed was illustrated to me on the River Inny in Ireland. I had been on a tope fishing expedition to the west coast in Ireland, in Co. Mayo with Jerry Airey and Nigel Newport. The ferry sailings back from Dublin to Holyhead gave us a full day free, and although we had been fishing for tope in shallow water for an entire week I didn't want to miss out on the chance to fish freshwater in Ireland.

We were due to stay just outside Dublin in bed and breakfast accommodation, then catch the ferry the following morning. Nigel had fished a pool on the Inny previously using bread, and had proclaimed every fish to be a five-pounder. It wasn't the two or three that he caught that made him want to return, it was the huge number he had seen rolling in the pool as evening drew to a close. I had never been there before. We had no bait, but on arrival in Mullingar we bought three loaves of bread.

As we drove down a narrow farm track with bushes scraping the car, we met a vehicle coming the other way. You normally meet tractors or herds of cows in Ireland, but rarely a car-load of other anglers. They told us that three anglers were already in the main pool and had been there since dawn. We pushed on anyway and fished just upstream from them. We caught nothing, so Nigel decided to poach their swim with some downstream casting. I kept well clear in case the sparks flew. As it was, the anglers were using very crude tackle, just watching the end of the rod top for a bream bite. Being Ireland they were catching some good bream, but not regularly. Around lunchtime they packed up, having taken about 180lb between them. Nigel commandeered what was left of their bait, a bucket of floating casters, and we moved in. We had groundbait, so using feeders and quivertip rods, we set about casting into the same area. There was an abundance of silkweed on the bottom, and any attempt to bump the feeder to let feed out resulted in the hookbait coming back with great strings of green stuff hanging from it. We lengthened the tail from hook to feeder and once it was cast into position we left it there. Apart from the odd tangle, the rigs stayed put. We hit a few fish, all scrapping well in the river current, and they were big fish—around $4\frac{1}{2}$–5lb apiece. This was the size of bream to reach a big weight with, but they weren't coming quickly enough, and we didn't have too much time. I tackled up a second rod, and so did Nigel and Jerry. With six rods all pumping casters into a confined area the inevitable happened. All the bream in the main pool swam over and got their heads down on the feed.

We weighed only what we thought were the largest fish, and the weight crept over 5lb to 5 10½oz, then 5lb 12oz, 5lb 14oz and finally, with a cheer, one of us broke the 6-lb barrier. It didn't stop there. The bites came faster, the third keepnet went out, and the top weight rose to 6lb 1oz, 6lb 2oz and 6lb 3oz—not small bream by river standards. The bag went well past the 100-lb mark, then 150, 175 until I estimated that we had topped 200lb! That's a lot of big bream in just a couple of hours. Jerry wandered off downstream, as he couldn't handle any more fish after the thirty-odd tope we had already caught. Neither Nigel nor I had any intentions of stopping, as we both realised that something special was happening. We pushed on without Jerry.

I estimated that we had passed 240lb, then about 280. It was getting dark and Jerry wanted to go back to get some food and sleep, but Nigel and I weren't going to pack up that close to 300lb. It was a weight neither

The author took one of his biggest river hauls when he fished in Ireland with Nigel Newport and Norman Wilkinson. Here Norman and Graeme display well over 250lb of river bream. As you can see, all the fish are laid on wet plastic sheeting, and will be returned straight after the photo.

of us had reached before in six hours, and this was our chance. If anything the bream fed even harder with the failing light, and it was a question of casting a feeder out, putting the rod in the rest, filling the feeder on the second rod, striking a bream on the first, leaving that rod in the rest while the hooked bream went off downstream, then casting out the second rod to fish while you played the first fish! It was fast fishing indeed.

We did the weighing in one session, passing the weighed bream back to an empty keepnet for a breather. It's always best to rest fish before photographing. I totted up the weights by torchlight, and with a shout gave our total—304lb! And each fish averaged a good 5lb. I am happy to say that all the fish went back with a smile on their faces, which is the way it should be. Later in the car we discussed the old breamer's fallacy that 'if you return a bream to the water, you'll never catch another bream all day'. What this means is that a returned fish will take the rest of the shoal with it. Yet had we not just seen the previous three anglers return 180lb of bream back to exactly the same swim before we moved in and hammered even more? That was a total of 484lb of bream from that one swim. It may be that a lost bream would normally race off downstream with the others following it. They are a shoal fish and spend most of their time together as a group, but in low-water conditions they would be unlikely to run upstream into the rapids and rocks, and while they could have swum downstream, the water was at summer level and only a foot or so deep. They probably just raced around the pool, then with nowhere to go just settled down again.

I don't believe that a lost fish will spook the rest of the shoal, except when the bream are about to settle down on the feed. It may take them a while to get their heads down, but after that I don't think a hand grenade would budge them. But if you hook and lose a bream that is the first to pick up the bait, I expect it might make the others nervous, and they might follow it away from the baited area if you lose it. Having said that, my big-game-fishing exploits do seem to confirm the theory. When I used to fish light tackle on the offshore banks of Bermuda for yellowfin tuna, a similar theory was held by the skippers. The Bermuda skippers are experts in the art of chumming or groundbaiting with anchovies to bring the big tuna near the boat. Often the first fish to show in the chum trail would be the little tunny, a fine sporty little fish that raced around grabbing the free offerings of fish chunks. These fish would range in size from about 5lb up to 10. The skippers refused to let me hook one of them until the yellowfins were really feeding heavily in the trail, as any fish initially hooked before the yellowfins were really hard on the feed would crash-dive through the depths, taking any nervous yellowfins with it. This was confirmed, as polaroid sunglasses enabled me to see everything that was happening. So perhaps there is something to it. But if I do lose a first bream, it certainly won't induce me to pack up!

Techniques

Having established that the bream is a lover of soft, mud-bottomed lakes, you would do well to concentrate your attentions on the leger. While I enjoy fishing on the float for this species, I think the fight they put up on my carbon match rod probably makes the fishing seem better than it is. Certainly floatfishing is not as productive as putting baits hard on the bottom. I have only taken a few fish 'on the drop', and that has been when there is a shoal hard on the feed. While they will hang around in shoals at mid water, or even near the surface, they rarely feed there, and the underslung mouth is indicative of their preference for bottom feeding.

The techniques for legering baits on the lake bed are numerous, and I certainly don't pretend to know them all. However, the few I mention here have stood me in good stead through a wide variety of fishing conditions, and resulted in some satisfying bags of fish. Bream aren't difficult to catch once they start to come, but it is often those small details like a change in terminal rigs that turn a frustrating day into a good one. You will also find these successful with many other species of fish, so the chances are good that you will hit *some* fish even if the bream aren't present.

Running Leger

This consists of a hook on the end, an arseley bomb or similar lead with a swivel mounted in it and a plastic leger stop. As with many things, the simplest rigs often catch the most fish. The idea of the running leger is that a fish can pick up the bait, and as it moves off, pull the line which slides unhindered through the lead's swivel eye. This in turn gives an indication at the angler's end, and you should have something to strike at. The plastic leger stop stops the lead sliding down on to the hookbait, and the length of line between this stop and the hook is called the tail. This tail can be

41

anything from 12in to 3ft long. Obviously with the tail at 12in, the fish moves a short distance before registering a bite. If the tail is 3ft long, it moves further before a bite is indicated.

If you have some long-distance casting to reach your intended swim, the force of the lead against the leger stop might make it skid down to the hook under power. At night you might not see this, but an experienced angler can tell by the speed of the lead through the air whether the stop has slipped. If in doubt, wind in and recheck. There are two ways to avoid this: You can either use two leger stops, butting one up against the other, or you can pinch a shot on the line in place of the leger stop. The disadvantage of using a shot in place of a plastic leger stop is that pinching it on the line with your teeth can fracture the line. You might then find that the lead cracks off on the cast or, worse still, that you break a fish off on the strike.

If you want to stop the lead with a shot, slide a tiny piece of silicon tube on the mainline first (your local tackle shop should have some) and then bite the shot on to that. It takes the edge off the pressure and can be backed by another length of silicon tube, this time about 2in longer, between the lead and the piece used as the stop. When you distance cast with a heavy lead, it pushes against the length of tube, and also cushions the effect of the casting power.

Link Leger

The next step would be to use a link leger. In this case the lead is tied on to another length of line so that it stands away from the mainline. I prefer this method, as it seems to give freedom of movement to a taking fish. The length of the link can be as little as four inches or as much as a couple of feet. It's best applied when there is an abundance of bottom weed that might clog the eye of the lead's swivel in the standard running leger. The problem of weed on the bottom can also be alleviated by the use of a balanced stiff tube to keep the swivel eye off the bottom. Some books classify this as a paternoster rig, but the mainline is still free running. Bream and tench anglers have been using balanced stiff tubes for years. The idea possibly came from anglers who actually glued pieces of cork around the top of the lead, so that when it sank to the bottom the lead would remain upright, thus keeping the swivel eye clear of weed. The stiff tube is merely an extension of this, and was originally made with a piece of sarkandas reed stem about 6in long. Now you can buy stiff or pliable plastic black tubing from either a tackle shop or a model shop, cut it to the required length, and balance one end with an insert of either cork or polystyrene. The average length of the tube would be about 6in, but

The author enjoys fishing fast water bream, and this catch of chub and bream came from the top weirpool of the Royalty Fishery on the Hampshire Avon. He used chest waders and put cheese on a link leger, casting upstream into the fast water.

In meres, the bream may be out in the deepest part of the lake. Use stiffer rods to get your swimfeeder or leger rig well out, and strike hard when you get a bite. Nylon line will stretch 10% of its length before it will break.

remember that this is used only for a link leger, and the length of the tube dictates the length of the link from lead to swivel.

Fixed Paternoster

If you have a heavy swimfeeder rig to cast you might want to dispense with leger stops altogether, and simply tie in a swivel where the stop is intended to be. Your lead or feeder would slide down on to this, and there would be no chance of slipping, no matter how hard you cast. My advice, however, would be still to use a 2in length of silicon tubing to cushion the shock of casting. Where big baits are being used for fish that are very confident when they take, the running leger rigs are my favourite. But if you have a water which is heavily fished, either by match fishermen or specimen hunters or both, you might want to use a fixed paternoster. With these any bite indication is almost immediate and you will need to concentrate in order to strike immediately. Matchmen use the fixed paternoster rigs for this reason. The fish might be finicky and an inch is all you are going to get as an indication.

The method I use for fixing the lead or feeder to the line is the four-turn water knot. You need a little movement before the fish feels any resistance, so make sure you don't fix the lead too close to your mainline. From six inches to about two feet is what you want. Again, the closer the lead is to the mainline, the more immediate your strike should be. The moment any bream feels the resistance of the lead it is likely to eject the bait, but on occasions they will actually hook themselves. They do this by dashing off in alarm when they feel the resistance. If your hook is small and chemically sharpened, the weight of the lead will hold the point in until you can strike. With bigger hooks and baits, I don't bargain on being so lucky!

The rig looks the same as the link leger, except that where the link leger offers a running lead, the paternoster has it fixed to the mainline. As well as fishing with the lead above the hook, you can make a paternoster with the lead below the hook. You simply tie in a barrel swivel to your mainline about 2ft from where the hook would be, then tie the lead on the end in place of the hook. Your hook link is then tied in where the lead would go, on a length of line shorter than the lead, usually about one third of the length. This hook link is tied directly on to the eye of the swivel.

Running Paternoster

This is a variant of the above rig, and it allows you to keep close contact with the lead by having a tight line. Instead of having a fixed hook link or tail, it is like a running leger. Start by making up your lead link with about 3ft of your mainline. On one end tie a barrel swivel and on the other your lead. Then thread your reel line through the top end of the barrel swivel, put on a leger stop with a 6–9in tail, then tie on your hook. It's as simple as that. The running paternoster is more suitable for larger baits like worms, bread or sweetcorn, while the fixed paternoster rigs are better for hitting twitchy bites on smaller bait sizes. If you are sitting by your rods, and strike at the first indication of a positive bite, you should hook all your fish cleanly in the mouth.

There is no real way to stop a bream taking the bait deep, but a couple of tips might minimise the problem. Most deep-hooked bream are caused by anglers using a long tail or hook link and failing to straighten it out after they have cast. The problem is accentuated with the length of the hooklink. For instance you may be fishing with a long hooklink, say 30ins. You cast out, the lead sinks to the bottom, but the hooklink lies in a heap on top of it. The bream comes along, picks up the bait, and without moving more than a few inches proceeds to eat it on the spot. The line is slack, so the angler has no idea what is happening until the bream moves off, after which it will be hooked deep. In the bream fishing trade these are called throaters. When you cast out, let the lead hit the bottom, then take two or three turns of the reel handle to drag the lead towards you and straighten out the tail or hooklink on the bottom. If the problem persists, it means that the bream are feeding very hard in a confined area, and you will have to shorten your hooklink in order to strike earlier. With fixed paternosters the problems are the same, but as long as you are tight to the lead, the bite should indicate well.

It is best to fish with a lead when the area you are fishing has been groundbaited heavily and the bream are thought to be present, either because of the clouding of the bottom as they root around in the mud, or because of bubbles rising to the surface, or by liners—fish that are moving through the swim generally prior to getting their heads down in earnest and feeding. They bump into the mainline, catching it with their fins, and obviously give you an indication at your rod. Striking has no effect, although occasionally you foulhook a fish. Liners may also mean that you have overcast the baited area, and the bream are moving inside you. By gently bumping your lead in with a few turns of the reel handle you can drag your hooklink on to the baited patch and your next bite should connect with a fish. It may sound difficult to try to distinguish a real bite from a liner, but the latter will drag your bobbin indicator, quivertip or swingtip round, and just as you are about to strike it will drop back to the original position. A normal bite should pull the indicator up and hold it there. Liners are not very difficult to distinguish, but you have to miss a few fish actually to experience what they feel like. The problem is accentuated when you are fishing across a deep channel in a gravel pit, with your bait lying on a sloping shelf on the opposite side of the channel. Your mainline will be suspended in the mid water of the channel and any fish running slightly on the deeper side of the shelf can bump into it, causing a false bite. There is no way round this, except to bump your bait down the shelf a bit further so that the bream find it before they find the line! To a lesser extent the rigid boom paternoster or running leger will hold the mainline off the bottom for a foot or so either side of the boom. This creates another area where the bream can bump the line. Again, there is no way round this as the idea of the boom is to suspend the line and swivel above weed anyway, but at least it's interesting to know why you might be missing fish.

Feeder Fishing

Of all the techniques employed in the pursuit and capture of bream, fishing the feeder must be the most productive. Swimfeeders now come in a wide variety of weights, shapes and sizes, with different methods of groundbait distribution. They come into their own when you want to introduce small quantities of feed into your swim gradually. With heavy pre-baiting for bream you are putting a lot of feed in all at once, and there is little point in putting more in with a swimfeeder. If the bream have moved on to a heavily baited patch you are going to catch them anyway, but the feeder builds a swim gradually. Pre-baiting is best done the day, or at the very latest the night before your intended session. It is unusual to get an immediate response from bombarding a swim with bait, then fishing it straight away. Therefore, if you intend to fish an area you have no experience of, or if you don't even know if bream can be caught there, then light feeding is best. If there are fish present, an immediate bombardment could frighten them away from the area. The introduction of groundbait and your intended hookbait via a swimfeeder may start them feeding.

The most common problem anglers face is that they leave the feeder in the water too long, and make the groundbait too stodgy. On a fast-flowing river you can get away with stodgy groundbait, as the action of the current will empty the feeder for you. But on a stillwater there is little point in having all that lovely bream food sealed up tightly in a plastic container! You should therefore cast out leaving the feeder no more than five minutes before bumping it in a foot or so.

The best type of feeder is called open-ended. As the name implies, it is not only full of holes to allow maggots and particles of groundbait to escape, but it is open for filling at either end. There are two ways to fill this type. First you can squeeze a plug of just groundbait into the top end (the end with the loop or swivel), fill the centre with your intended hookbait—maggots, casters, corn etc—then plug the other end up with another wedge of groundbait. You should make sure that the bottom plug of groundbait isn't squeezed in too tightly, as you want the contents to spill out slowly. The alternative is to mix your hookbait in with the main mix of groundbait and just fill the feeder from top to bottom with it. The art is to mix the groundbait so that it is just damp and holds together lightly when you squeeze it. If it is too wet, it gets stodgy and sticks in the feeder. If it is too dry, it flies out on the cast. Trial and error is the best way to gain experience. Mix just a small amount first, so that if it doesn't turn out right you can dry it with further groundbait or dampen it with water. It is better to have it too dry than too wet.

Another feeder to try is called the frame feeder. This is a cone- or pear-shaped mesh feeder around which you simply squeeze a handful of groundbait. Follow the above advice for mixing the consistency correctly, as you want it to break up either on impact, or preferably at the bottom. The advantage with frame feeders is that you can introduce a good deal more feed than with enclosed feeders. Some anglers start a session with a frame feeder, moulding very large balls around it, then dropping the quantities and using an open-ended feeder once the bream have settled in the swim. The disadvantage of this method is that by squeezing extra large balls of groundbait to the feeder you either overload the rod during the cast or simply cast too far. There may also be a problem with directional casting if you don't squeeze the same amount of groundbait on to the frame each time. Dropping groundbait like this accentuates the problems of line bites, as the feed is all over the place. So although the frame feeder has its place, I would suggest that beginners stick with the open-ended variety before moving on to it.

The block-end feeder is plastic, and is designed to distribute samples of hookbait into the swim. It has a fixed plastic cap at one end, and a hinged cap at the other. You merely fill the feeder with maggots, hemp, worm etc and cast out. Remember when using live baits like maggots that they soon wriggle free of the holes, so there is no need to 'bump' this type of feeder along the bottom to empty it. Lively maggots empty themselves, as do small worms, but hemp and caster will need a foot or two of twitching along the bottom to help them free of the feeder. If you want to use larger-particle seed baits like sweetcorn, remember to enlarge the feeder holes by drilling or melting them with a hot nail. Make sure you bait your hook first and then fill the feeder. Doing it the other way round will see your feeder emptied while you fiddle about trying to get a couple of maggots to stay on the hook. Fill the feeder while holding it over the bait container so as to waste less. If your maggots come with bran to reduce the chances of sweating, don't put the bran in the feeder, otherwise it clogs the holes and prevents the maggots from wriggling out.

The block-end feeder is effective and comes in large sizes, but the best type is called the Drennan feeder. These are smaller cylinders of plastic, and they too can have their holes enlarged for faster distribution of live baits like maggots. They come in a variety of sizes, they are camouflaged with a green tinge and, being narrower with the weights at one end, they cast like bullets. They are ideal for fishing estate waters or meres where the deepest area of water is likely to be towards the centre, and where every yard of casting distance is critical. You can adjust the weight at the base of the feeder using swan shot or put on a bomb weight for long-distance fishing. The cap fits snugly over the end, and they are altogether a handy feeder for giving you that edge on the fish. For much of your fishing, you might want to fish the feeder on a link, like the links described in the sections on lead techniques. I use the four-turn water knot for fishing small feeders, but I prefer a running leger much of the time.

Two problems can occur when feeder fishing. The first is 'bumping off' a bream. This simply means that a heavy feeder limits the amount of shock absorption you get with nylon monofilament line. It is said that a nylon fishing line stretches some 10 per cent of its length. Bearing in mind that the feeder may only be two feet from the hook, if you have cast thirty yards, the maximum cushioning effect is between your rod top and the feeder—over 2.9 yards. Between the hook and the weight of the feeder the bream has two feet (or less), which means that if you hold them hard they can plunge sharply, and the sudden shock breaks the line between hook and feeder. This is even worse when you are fishing with a weaker hooklink than the mainline, say 2-lb hooklink to 5-lb mainline. For this reason, I like to play out all the bream hooked on a feeder rod by using my wrist rather than lining up the butt along my forearm. If I adopt the latter position I have the strength of my forearm, which is less likely to give under the pressure of a sudden lunge by the bream. If I play the fish out using just my wrist, it is much weaker and therefore more likely to give under any sudden strain. It makes your wrist ache, but I was taught this technique by a matchman who couldn't afford to bump off any bream in a match. Bream aren't the hardest scrappers in the world, but I wouldn't want to bump one off the hook by hauling it too hard and then weigh my net of fish at 98-lb!

The other problem is that using a fixed paternoster and feeder, if I should break a fish off it might have to drag the feeder around, eventually snagging up and dying. A few anglers use 3-lb line straight through with a fixed paternoster, but I use nothing less than 5-lb, and I use a hooklink below the feeder. Thus should a breakage occur, the fish is free of the feeder, and is unlikely to snag up. The swimfeeder is of paramount importance in a bream angler's arsenal, but always remember to bump it along the bottom occasionally. Bream that are just browsing through a swim may be attracted by the sudden movement of a feeder and pick up the angler's bait. Also, the feeder that is bumped along a foot or so will leave a trail of groundbait and hook particles behind it, and the hookbait is anything from 3ft to 6in behind the feeder, so bumping it along ensures that the groundbait and your hookbait are lying in the same area.

Floatfishing

While feeder fishing is the most productive of all bream fishing techniques, floatfishing must be the most enjoyable. There are so many variations of floats and shotting patterns that I intend to list only the very basics. There are other books specifically about floatfishing that the bream angler can look to if he wants to progress further.

The object of bream fishing is to get hookbaits hard on the bottom. Apart from fast-river bream, the species is more likely to be taken hard on the bottom than at mid water. You therefore need a float capable of taking

Big bream like these can fall to a wide variety of techniques and baits. This bag came from the river Inny in Ireland.

Above: Weirpools, with their higher oxygen content and cooler temperatures in summer, are natural holding areas for most species.

Below: For many youngsters, the thrill of hooking a bream can start them on the road to success. With a broad flank, even a 3-lb bream can look like a specimen fish to a young angler.

The author with a catch of fast-water bream and a single chub, taken on the float using sweetcorn as bait.

Top left: If the water you intend fishing is hard fished by both match anglers and pleasure fishermen, use a bait tray to give you instant access to a choice of hookbaits.

Top right: Unhooking big bream is no problem if you use a plastic disgorger or artery forceps. If your fish is continually deep hooked on leger tackle, simply shorten up the length of the 'tail', and hit the bites earlier.

Left: The best time to use casters is when they are just going a golden brown. Kept in the fridge, they can send bream wild when mixed into the groundbait.

Facing page: The author uses Mukluk chest waders to trot a float down this stretch of the Royalty fishery on the Hampshire Avon. Even traditionally fast waters like this are becoming home to increasing bream shoals.

Canals in winter are worth trying after snow has fallen. Stillwaters may be frozen, but slow-moving canals can often remain ice-free a bit longer, and give the angler a chance of some fish.

Below: Fishing for hybrids can provide great sport on light match tackle. Today the modern angler travels to Ireland to get the best hybrid fishing in Europe.

Slow-moving rivers may have some limited boat traffic, but should also have marginal weed like these lilies. The channel in the centre will be deeper which is why the lilies aren't growing there, so once you find some weed, you have a guide to depths.

An angler settles in for a good session as the sun sets, and the lake stills as the wind drops. By dawn he should have several fish in the net; sunset to midnight and dawn being the two main feeding periods.

Techniques

These two anglers have waded out to the edge of a loch's dropoff in order to floatfish. Wear a bait apron for terminal gear and hookbait, and peg the keepnet close by your side

a fair bit of weight to cock it, yet adaptable to all the conditions of fishing either rivers or stillwaters. Of the many varieties around, I suggest that you should start out with the waggler. As far as I am aware the term 'waggler' merely means a float that is attached through the bottom end only, so waggling around when you first drop it in the water or twitch it with the rod. Waggler fishing is designed to beat the problems of drift on a stillwater or current drag in a slow-moving river, where a downstream wind will pull the float too fast and move it out of position.

Some wagglers are designed for long-distance fishing and can take two or three swan shot as cocking weights. These are the long-stem bodied wagglers obtainable in your tackle shop. Some are used for slow-moving rivers, some for deeps, some for shallows. Some have single stems with no bodies. Others are slim-tapered, yet others are short and dumpy. One of the better floats is called a Driftbeater, and suits rough choppy conditions which might drag an ordinary float out of position. Two swan shot are locked either side of the bottom float ring, and another shot, either swan or bb, is pinched about a foot from the hook. The float is cocked so that this bottom shot is lying on the lake bed, partially anchoring the float to the bottom. When a bite occurs the float will slide away rather than dive

Go Fishing for Bream

By selecting a lake not affected by floodwater, the author and Nigel Newport took over 100lb of bream and three bonus pike on float tackle. Approach your bream fishing with forethought and you stand every chance of making a big bag.

straight down. If the bream are in particularly finicky mood, the anchoring shot can be moved as close as a couple of inches to the hook, thereby giving an immediate bite indication. This rig would use a bodied waggler, with the bulk of the buoyancy in the bottom half of the float. The float tip might be marked with a bright paint to allow you to see the bite more easily in rough conditions.

For smaller bream, say fish under 2lb, and in less breezy conditions, you can use a lighter waggler with a slimmer body, still using two shot for locking either side of the float, say bb in size. Then halfway down the depth pinch a couple of number 4 or 6 shot, and use a dust shot as the

A Hampshire gravel pit offers good bream fishing. In a good angler's hands, the pole can outfish a running line at close range.

anchor lying on the bottom. With this rig, and in the quieter water, you can actually cast slightly upwind of the baited area, and induce a take by letting the dust shot slowly drag bottom. Whereas in rough weather you need the bodied waggler to provide enough buoyancy to use a heavier anchor shot, a slowly drifting bait can sometimes get the extra takes in calmer weather. I think the bait movement in the clearer water actually attracts the bream's attention. In rough weather the bottom may have silt stirred up in suspension, and a drifting bait is missed by the fish.

In dead calm weather, particularly if the lake is of the estate type with a regular level bed, I like a straight-stem waggler. These can be ten inches long, occasionally more, and they are shotted down to leave just a tip of float showing. If a strong ripple is on the water they bob underneath too much and you need to change the bodied waggler, but in calm conditions they not only cast well but give a delicate bite indication. Keep most of the shot bulked either side of the float ring and place a dust shot about 12in from the hook. Don't keep it hard on the lake bed but about a foot off, thus stabilising the float more.

Go Fishing for Bream

For river work, providing the current flow is steady like that on the Thames, you can still use a waggler. The problem here is that these slower rivers have substantial boat traffic, and this in turn may push the bream over to the far bank or near to islands. The waggler is ideally suited to take a heavy enough shotting pattern to get it near the swims, but the problem is maintaining control over it. Standard river trotting techniques generally entail a float attached top and bottom. The line goes from your rod top to the top of the float, and if a downstream wind puts a belly into the line, thus dragging the float faster than the pace of the current, you can mend the line by picking it off the surface and laying it back upstream. The waggler float is attached by the bottom end only and therefore the slightest movement on the rod top will bob the float under, giving you a false bite. A few anglers grease the reel line and don't mind bobbing the float under in order to mend the line, but in my opinion the moment you start tweaking the float about is just the moment when a big bream inspects the bait below. If that twitches too, it is likely to ignore it. Another problem if you degrease the line and fish it below the surface is that the current is not always constant across the entire width of the river. It seems to be sod's law that the current inside the swim is faster than at the far bank, and the increase in flow also pulls the waggler under! Obviously you should do your best to pick a swim with a constant flow rate across its width but if you can't do this it is better to switch to a quivertip, using a very light test curve model, and not to bother with floatfishing at all, particularly on a hard-fished match water where any mending of the line or bait disturbance is likely to be treated with disdain by the bream. As I said earlier, bream are not difficult to catch, but they're not stupid!

When casting wagglers on stillwaters, you will invariably need to sink the line to avoid the problem of surface drift dragging the float under continually. To do this you degrease the line with a pad of cotton wool soaked in some washing-up liquid. I always take a small container in my tackle box for such occasions. To sink the line you must first cast beyond your intended baited area, sink your rod top under the water and wind fast for several turns of the reel. Stop when you think the float is still short of the swim, and let it pop up to show you where it is. You can then inch it in slowly until it sits directly over your baited patch.

The tip is to cast hard to get the waggler flying out past the swim, but stop it before it hits the water by putting your finger on the lip of the spool. This has the effect of making the hookbait zip past the float so that when they hit the water you will have the line from hook to float lying in a straight line. In all but the roughest weather, you can actually see the double blip as float and bait hit the water. If you don't see those two blips on the surface, wind in and you will probably find the hook and shot tangled around the float. The float would still cock, as the weight is below the waggler, but you would be unaware of the wasted time until you wound in.

If your intention is to try for the fast-water bream, then you need a bodied Avon float, which is altogether different in design and capable of taking a lot of shot. I like to spread mine along the top two thirds of trace from float to hook, with a single number 4 or even a bb about fifteen inches from the hook. With such a good weight to stabilise the terminal tackle in the current you can hold back the float in the fast current and let the bait precede it downstream. If you don't hold back, the current will put a bow in the line and the fish may see it before the hookbait. Remember that the current on a river is slower near the river bed than anywhere else, because of the water's friction with the gravel, mud or rocky bottom. Avon floats come in a variety of sizes, and as the largest hookbait for this fast-water bream fishing should be a grain of sweetcorn, you should keep the float size as low as fishing conditions allow. There is no point in missing out on finicky bites by using tackle that is too heavy.

On some faster rivers there will be an area of deep water close under the bank. As a rule of thumb, for any distance you can hold your rod—say a 12ft matchrod—out at 90 degrees to the bank, I would use a stick float. These take a lot less shot, are not built up by any extra body, and are therefore very sensitive to bites. They need to be shotted carefully, allowing just a tip to show, barely $\frac{1}{4}$in. You can also hold this tackle back, but I find letting it run through where there is a constant flow will often pick off the bream. Stick floats are better suited to roach, dace and grayling fishing, but a heavier wire-stemmed stick float can also be used to take bream.

There are many options open to the float angler after bream. Models like zoomers, sliders, duckers and darts can all be used, but I feel that a selection of wagglers suffices for most stillwater trips, and a couple of sizes of Avons and sticks will do for the rivers.

The last type of float of use to the bream angler is the sliding float. This is used when you want to floatfish in water that has a greater depth than the length of your rod. The average match float rod would be 12ft, and a good depth to cast into would be 10ft or less. Above that, you would need to stand on your tackle box to get the length from hookbait to float correct, and that's just not practical! The sliding float has a ring at the bottom and a ring near the top, but to the side. I even bend the lower eyelet of my sliding float at right angles to make it slide up the line better. You are going to need something to stop the float at the required depth and this is done with a stop knot. Some anglers like to use a tiny plastic bead between the top ring of the float and the stop knot, otherwise a very small stop knot will slide through it. Tackle shops today stock a tiny rubber stopper that can be put on the line to act in the same way as the stop knot, and this can be slid up and down the line without weakening it. The age-old problem of stop knots was that if you tied them too tightly the line was weakened every time you slid them up and down the line with your nail. Eventually the line would part under pressure, and it always happened when you had a decent fish just out of netting range!

My opinion is that if you have water over 10ft deep you should use leger tactics anyway, and I rarely use the sliding rig unless I want a delicate bite indicator signalling bites on the edge of a deep-water ledge or over an area of deep water where rocks might prevent a good bite on the leger. Some of the Irish loughs are like this, and you may break off on the strike as the line catches round a rock. Then the sliding float is master of the situation. You can also rig a waggler float as a slider, by running the line through the bottom eye and using either the rubber stopper or a stop knot, either of which should be small enough to pass through the rod rings.

One of the most interesting days I recall on the float was spent at a small lake near Ballinamore, Co. Leitrim. I had been over for a five-day stint researching fishing articles with Nigel Newport, and as can happen in the Emerald Isle, the weather turned nasty. The late Denis Breen was our host, and he tried his best to put us on to some fish, even down to getting his other clients out fishing lakes just to get some bait in. It saved us wasted fishing time, but it transpired that the cold-water flush-through had put them right off the feed. Most of the large lakes and loughs in this, the lakeland region of Ireland, are linked by streams, ditches or rivers. That means that any excess water running down the system effectively puts an end to any fishing from lake to lake. All we had been doing was racing around trying different waters in the hope that one would fish, when in fact the conditions were the same in all of them.

I realised what had happened, and opted for any lake that was on a hillside, set in a rising piece of ground or generally without any ditch or stream draining into it. Any excess water going into the lake would be purely from surface run-off. Temperatures would be more consistent, colour from the peat ground draining into the lake would be minimal, and such a water might be fishable. Being Ireland's lakeland, you can imagine how many bodies of water there were marked on the Central Fisheries Board map of the region! Add to that another 50 per cent that were too small to be marked, or had not yet even been discovered, and you can see how difficult it was to locate one that was not linked by drainage.

However, Denis found us one, and it really was small by Irish standards, perhaps about 8 acres. It had a couple of wooden fishing platforms on it, and that evening saw us both down there examining it. The first thing that struck me was that it was gin clear, and the margins were fringed with lilies. The lilies were bumped every so often and the reed beds juddered every ten minutes. It looked as though bream were in there cleaning off after spawning, so we plumbed the depth (around 3ft, two rod-lengths out), put in some light feed and floatfished. The reason for floatfishing was that the bottom felt as though it was littered with lily roots, and as the margins were already showing lilies unfolding on the surface, the chances were that in high summer the entire lake surface would be matted with their leaves. If we legered, the hookbaits might be covered by newly opened leaves, and we didn't have the time to drag out and pre-bait the swim.

Maggots and caster brought only rudd, and breadflake only larger rudd, although Nigel thought he bumped a bream off on the strike. As night fell the bream started to roll, their black backs breaking the oily surface like a school of dolphin. They were there but wouldn't feed. Before we left we heaved in a mix of brown crumb, white loaves, maggots, casters squashed up and some worm extract. It looked and smelt disgusting, but might just make the bream feed. If it didn't, the lake would be polluted with worm extract!

We grabbed no more than a few hours' sleep and at 3am we left for the lake. By 4.15am we were set up and straining to see the float tops in the low-light conditions. I thought I saw mine drifting to one side, lifted to recast and found a bream attached! It was soon in the net, but few others came, despite an extra helping of maggot. I changed to lobworm, and the float sank beneath the surface from the added weight of the worm. I wound in, bit off a shot, and cast out again. This time the float cocked with about an inch of its orange tip showing, then promptly slid under again. Cursing, I lifted to recast—and a bream was on it. It's not often I get so lucky twice in a row!

After this Nigel changed to lobworm tail, and hit a fish. Then I had a four-pounder and they started to come with reasonable regularity. Unfortunately the introduction of the extra maggots had pulled in the rudd population and the pike—only small jacks—weren't far behind. The first pike came to a large lobworm on Nigel's rod, and thrashed off through the margin lilies, the line cutting them off neatly so they popped on to the surface. After 10am the swim went slack, which gave me time to throw a plug around. I extracted another two pike, then the bream came again. There were no monsters, which was just as well because you could feel the line catch on a lily stem or root, then twang free as a fighting bream moved around. I'm sure that if we had been leger fishing we would not only have had fewer bites, but possibly have lost more fish in the roots. As it was we could hold our match rods high over our heads to keep as little line in the water as possible, pumping the bream slowly to the surface. When Denis returned to help us weigh in, the catch was about 111lb between the two of us, and that is still one of my better bream catches on the float. I aim to top 100lb on a float. Many people must have done it already in Ireland, but I haven't yet, so its something to look forward to, and a very real possibility if bottom fishing is tricky. Any fish on the float is entertaining, and worth three on the quivertip or swingtip.

Pole Fishing

The angler interested in catching just any size bream might try pole fishing. Used mainly in matches where small fish are required for a good total weight, it is a delicate method of presenting a bait that is attractive to all fish, not just small species. Match anglers would not set out to catch a fish as large as a bream using pole tackle, but such is the flexibility of a good pole rig that it often happens in matches.

Pole fishing is a specialised technique about which others have written in length. Popularised through the publicity generated by Continental match successes, the pole is now an integral part of the British matchman's armoury. The pole is a light carbon, graphite or glass and carbon mix that is joined together in sections, reaching out over the water to the top of the swim. There is no reel attached to the butt, and the angler fishes with either a crook or an elastic fixed directly from the pole tip to the terminal tackle.

When fishing with a crook, small fish are the intended quarry, and a length of strong line, say 5lb, is tied from the tip to the float, which is on a lighter link of line. When a fish is hooked, it is swung out immediately on the pole, disengaging the odd section until the fish is swung to hand. If the small fish are found in a swim close to the angler's bank they can literally be popped out like corks, using a shorter pole with which they can be swung straight to the angler's hand at chest height. Problems arise when you hook a larger fish, as although the pole will bend significantly, it can give no further line than the length from tip to float. If a big bream is hooked it will swim away, breaking off.

The other method, which alleviates this problem somewhat, is to use elastic in the tip end of the pole, that acts as a shock absorber. This elastic comes in a variety of strains, and matchmen carry about four sizes. It can range from 12oz or less to 1½-lb or more. It must be remembered that this is the breaking strain *after* all the elasticity has been taken out of the length—and that can be quite considerable. A variation of the single strand of elastic is the twisted shock absorber. The variation in breaking strains that can be achieved by varying the lengths of twists is almost limitless, and this method is ideal for bream fishing when used in conjunction with heavier pole rigs. A water knot can be used to join the elastic to the terminal gear. Now when you hook a bream and it moves off, you can have yards of stretch in the elastic shock absorber to tire it out. You can also shorten the length of the pole as the fish comes closer to the bank, still keeping it at an angle to wear the fish out. This elastic absorber has been used by matchmen to take very big fish on lines as light as 1-lb breaking strain. A double-figure carp is by no means a rare capture on such tackle, and bream can be fished quite effectively when they are in a finicky mood.

The terminal rigs are kept on winders, so all you do is unwind them and connect them to the elastic. Use the heaviest float and shotting pattern you can, and use a larger hook than the matchmen use, say a 12 with a single grain of sweetcorn, or an 18 with double red maggot or double caster. I would not use single maggot or caster as this only gives bites from the unwanted smaller fish. I would keep the shot spread down the length of the line rather than under the float as is traditional. This gets the hookbait down to the bottom more quickly and reduces the chance of a slower-sinking bait being taken by unwanted smaller fish. Pole fishing would not be the most popular way to tackle bream, and I would limit its use to hard-fished British waters that have regular matches on them. There is no need for it in Ireland, where the fish are caught less and can therefore be taken on heavier line.

I have seen pole fishermen produce the goods so often that I know it is an effective method. There is no need to lay out a vast fortune on the purchase of several poles. Ask your local tackle dealer to sell you an average-length pole, primarily with big fish in mind (3lb or so), and stock up with no more than three different floats and pole winders for different conditions. Then you have the basic outfit and can pick off shy-biting bream when traditional tactics fail.

Tackle

Bream fishing can become fairly specialised, particularly if you want to be successful. There are of course occasions when a shoal of bream decides to take up residence in front of you, and get their heads down, and you can catch them easily. This happened on the river Inny in Ireland, where I saw three anglers fishing the same swim, a bend in the river with rapids above and below. The shoal was on a spawning migration and had bottled up in a pool. The fishermen were casting swimfeeders loaded with maggots and casters into the far corner of the pool, putting their heavy fibreglass rods in forked sticks and waiting for the whole rod top to pull round. It made me wonder why I had paid good money for a couple of delicate carbon quivertip rods, designed to register the tiniest bite!

However, I have no doubt at all that over a whole season, covering a dozen different situations and venues, my equipment would outfish them. Armed with good equipment and the right techniques, you could do the same. There is no need to go for the most expensive tackle on the market, and the tackle mentioned here would probably be termed 'middle of the road' equipment.

Rods

You cannot really fish efficiently with two float rods, but you can with a pair of feeder rods. I therefore advise purchasing just one three-section float rod, 12 or 13ft long, of carbon, or carbon/glass construction. You may pick up a secondhand one, but even new they can be bought for between £60 and £100. It may seem a lot, but for a light float rod you can hold all day, you'll find the outlay worthwhile. I have a Normark float road that I built myself, which could be regarded as on the light side for breaming, but at least I get a good scrap from a three-pounder.

Tackle

Staggering under a load of tackle he didn't use, and a tackle box full of rocks, Essex angler Jerry Airey is caught by Graeme's camera. Keep your tackle to the minimum, but your bait and groundbait to the maximum!

The tackle company Shimano field an excellent range of match rods, but go into your local tackle shop and put them together. Their twin-power tubular models range from 12 to 14ft and weigh from 4.5 to 5.6oz. These are top of the range and will be priced up to £145 or so. The power loop X tubular is a cheaper model running from 12 to 15ft and weighing from 4.5 to 6.5oz. So the more you pay, the lighter the rod you will get. On stillwaters you will be putting the rod in a rest, but for trotting a waggler or Avon float down a river you will be holding the rod all the time, so get the lightest you can afford. The standard power loop series of Shimano match rods range from 11 to 15ft and 4.5 to 6.6oz. They are priced from about £80 to £100. I see no reason to look further than the Shimano match rods.

For general leger and swimfeeder fishing I use the cheaper rods marketed by Ryobi Masterline. Years ago I had an old Ivan Marks Harrier feeder rod that took a screw-in quivertip or swingtip. I caught some incredible bags on it and still have it. The only problem with a screw-in quivertip was that it dog-legged over under tension, unlike the more

Go Fishing for Bream

This is how the author fishes two quivertip rods. The left rod is kept short in the rod rest and is cast slightly to the left of the swim. The right rod is extended out on the rests and is cast to the right. To minimise crossed lines when you hook a fish, degrease both lines with washing up liquid so they sink to the bottom. The hooked fish will then clear the other rod.

progressive curve of a spliced-in quivertip. Their Avon quivertip is a touch soft for heavy feeder fishing, but as a general all-round bream leger rod it suits my needs. It has the added advantage of two separate tops, one to make it a standard Avon, the other the quivertip. This rod is equipped with sliding black reel fittings and comes in either an abbreviated EVA handle or traditional cork. I did have the EVA handle but found that the reel slips round the butt, as bream fishing gets pretty sticky when you are feeding groundbait regularly. Get the cork-handled version, which stays drier. Apart from the spliced-in quivertip, which sports small black stand-off guides, the other guides are also all lined.

It may seem too simple to go with just one float rod and two leger, but it's all I use, and quite a few bream have crossed my landing net while using them. Some anglers say it is impossible to fish two quivertips for bream, as tangles occur. I disagree. All you do is cast your first rod to the left side of the swim (assuming you are a right-handed caster). Then cast your second rod to the right or centre of the swim. When you place this second rod in the rest, just extend the quivertip about 6in past the first, as though it were fishing on the outside of the first rod. Then when you strike to play a fish you'll have no tangles—except when you get a bite from another bream on the other rod, as has happened to me a few times!

Reels

In my opinion, there is only one make of reel for all coarse fishing situations, and that's the new Aero range by Shimano. I used a closed-faced reel for a lot of my fishing, but I have been so taken with the casting ability of the Aero range that I use their reel for trotting a float as well. It gives perfect casting with the minimum of weight and ultra-smooth delivery of line. The first few times I used an Aero match for floatfishing I lost three waggler floats in the bushes of the opposite bank. In fact they cast so well you have to reduce your casting impetus to reach the required spot. Their unique line lay is due to the long, tapered, shallow spool and the special spool oscillation at two speeds. On the larger 4500GT for instance, it lays seven coils parallel, then four diagonally.

The Aero Match 2000 has a gear ratio of 4.7 to 1, takes 100 yards or more of 2-lb test and is ideal for floatfishing. The Aero 2500M has a 6.2 to 1 recovery rate, and the larger spool takes 180 yards of 6-lb test. I would use this for feeder fishing. These would cost about £50–£60 at the time of writing. Another somewhat dumpy model that has proved popular is the Biomaster range. It features the front drag and the 2000X has a 4.7 to 1 line recovery rate and takes over 300 yards of 5-lb line—more than enough for long-distance feeder or leger fishing.

Those who enjoy the ease of line control of a closed-face reel should try the Ryobi Mastermatch. It weighs just 8oz, has a corrosion-resistant body and features an extra-wide graphite spool to eliminate line bedding when fighting a fish. The one-touch, non-slip line release knob is positive, while chenille trimming on the spool eliminates line trapping, a problem I had on another make of closed-face reel.

There are many other makes and models of reels, but these are the ones I consider to be the best for the job, without damaging the wallet too much.

Lines

I use only one line, the Maxima Chameleon in either 4- or 5-lb test. For lighter hooklinks when floatfishing, Bayer Perlon is good, but quite frankly if you asked six different matchmen what make of hooklink line they used you would probably get six different answers. Your local tackle shop would doubtless advise you on the most popular line in the 2-lb or less range. I have used Maxima for probably twenty years, and the only other line that comes near it is Ande tournament in green. This is an American line that I use almost exclusively in 12–130lb test, and nothing else can touch it. But for breaming, the 4- or 5-lb Maxima does the trick.

Keepnets

These will probably be a thing of the past in twenty years' time. Pressure on angling stocks is increasing all the time, and you cannot blame anglers for wanting to record a creditable catch they have made. The only times I use a keepnet are when working on features for magazines or illustrations for books, when you need a catch shot to illustrate a point. Much of the time I simply release each fish as I catch it, weighing, recording and photographing it when necessary.

If you do want to retain bream in a keepnet you should first buy the biggest you can afford. Mine is about 14ft long, and I have another of 20ft, consisting of two sewn together. It should have a wide neck, or opening. I have heard of new keepnets that feature a zipper in the bottom to allow the catch to be emptied easily rather than crashing them from one end of the net to the other. Of course with the zipper net, you should make sure you zip the end closed before you start putting fish in, otherwise they'll swim straight out the other end!

It is important that it should be pegged out in the water so that it doesn't collapse on the fish. I have also seen nets half out of the water at the open end purely because the angler doesn't want to get off his seat to put a bream in the net. It is better to get as much of the net under water as possible. Fish breath through water, not air. Try to peg the end of the net with a stick or with a rock with a piece of cord attached. Don't put a rock into the bottom of the net to hold it taut, otherwise the fish will be damaged when you bring the net in.

I've weighed and photographed plenty of bags of bream, some of them large fish to over 6lb, and I can honestly say that the following method gets the photograph, but minimises the stress to the fish. It takes two anglers and a spare keepnet. Invariably my big-bream catches happen with Nigel Newport, the manager of Tackle Up in my home town of Fleet. If we have one, two or three nets of bream we do the weighing in stages. You simply cannot properly weigh and photograph a bag of 60lb or more in one go, as you risk leaving the fish out of the water too long. If you have a good net of bream, they are going to come out fighting, as they have regained strength in the net. We peg out the empty keepnet, then shorten up one of the nets with fish in it. Nigel reaches in, and picks out five or six bream, placing them in the weigh sling, which I am holding inside the net ring. They are weighed and then transferred to the empty net. The weight is written down. When the first net has been emptied, we move to another,

This is how not to put your keepnet in the water. Half the rings are out of the water, and in hot, dry summers bream will become stressed. Better to walk out and peg the net in deeper water, even if it means you have to get up every time you want to put a fish in it. The welfare of the fish should come before your own comfort.

Another bream in the net for the author. If you aren't intending to photograph a bag of bream, just release them as you catch them.

repeating the process and putting the weighed fish in the now empty first keepnet. That way the fish are out of the water for no more than about sixty seconds, and they can recover in the empty keepnet.

After totting up the weights, we lay out a large sheet of plastic, avoiding any slope on the ground. Sometimes we lay a couple of rod holdalls on either side of the plastic to keep the fish from sliding off. That done, the cameras are primed and placed on clean towelling, sometimes mounted and pre-focused on a tripod and rigged to a bulb air release if nobody is about to help us get the shots. The nets are shortened up in the water, slowly lifting the bottom end until all the catch is in the top two rings. Then we lift them out straight on to the plastic. The fish are spread out, but the keepnets are left over their heads for thirty seconds to quieten them. Then the pictures are taken. If the catch is around 40–80lb we both pick the whole lot up in the plastic sheeting and carry them to the water. It's essential to get them into the water and then sort them out so that they swim away. Only by adhering to this routine are we able to get 'bag' photographs without risk to the fish. You get pretty wet and slimy, but the exercise is worthwhile when you see the bream swim away. Our largest photo session was 304lb of bream, but even then we did about 250lb first and returned them before completing the other job.

Landing Nets

These are essential if you don't want to drop fish by trying to pull them up to your hand. The latter is all right with 1-lb skimmer, but a 5-lb fish can still plunge away and either pop the line or tear the hook out. You don't need a 30-in carp net, and I don't like the circular 'dish-pan' matchman's net. A triangular net with an 18-in rim is best. If it is deep, shorten it by tying it up with spare line.

If you are using a lighter hooklink—say 2lb—you need to net the fish as soon as possible. If you watch when you hook bream, they occasionally boil on the surface. Try to keep your rod high, and the fish should stay on the surface all the way to the net. As long as you use a short pumping action with the rod and keep the bream's head coming towards you it's possible to stretch out with a full extension on your landing net pole and net it quickly. Don't try to lift it out of the water at full stretch. All you will do is buckle the landing net handle. Slide it in, hand over hand, and grasp the net frame or mesh to unhook the fish.

Bream are best lifted out by placing a finger and thumb either side of the base of the pectoral fin and holding the fish vertically. Once unhooked, place them straight in the keepnet. Modern landing nets have a base of soft mesh to avoid damaging the fish. I have a net at least fifteen years old and refuse to change it, as it brings me luck! It must have had a thousand or more fish slide over its rim, but I will only change it when it's rotten and a 7-lb bream drops through the bottom!

Hooks

I've little to say about hooks, as this is largely a matter of personal choice. If you are match-orientated you'll be talking in terms of maggots and casters, which means hook sizes 18–12. If you are after big bream you'll want sweetcorn, flake or lobworms, which means anything from a size 10 up to a 4. The best range for sharp hooks that I have found is produced by Partridge of Redditch. I recently changed to the specimen hooks, which are chemically sharpened, and have had a definite increase in hook-ups. Especially useful are their eyed hooks in sizes 16–10, which I use for maggots or bunches of worms. The only problems occur when you fish rocky bottoms like those of the big Irish loughs. They are fine while they are sharp, but if they catch a rock, the point could turn over. Check your points regularly under such conditions, and if in doubt, change the hook. In clear water, when float-fishing wagglers in shallow estate lakes or meres, try to use a gold hook for maggots, either white or bronze. The hook blends in with the

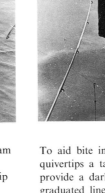

The quivertip should be part of a bream angler's arsenal in fast water fishing. You can see the bend in these quivertip rods as Nigel Newport fishes a fast stretch of Ireland's mighty River Shannon. Bites will register as a sharp knock forward or a slack line drop-back bite.

To aid bite indication when using quivertips a target board can be made to provide a dark background with graduated lines, to let you see how far the bites are taking the tip round. They make concentration much easier.

colour of the bait more and might just tip the balance in your favour if the fish are a bit tentative.

Swingtips and Quivertips

Swingtips are used to indicate bites from fish moving away or coming towards you, and are very sensitive. They are screwed into the tip eye of your leger rod. You cast out, let the bait settle and then tighten up so that the swingtip hangs slightly off the vertical. It will either twitch up or drop back, depending on which way the fish is feeding. Swingtips are very good for stillwater, but useless for rivers, as the current simply drags the tip out straight. The other disadvantage is that casting can be inaccurate, and distance is definitely cut because of the excess friction. They can be adjusted to suit windy conditions or surface drag by adding tiny coils of lead wire to the tip ring. They can be bought or made from varying weights. Try to buy a model with a soft silicon tube attachment. If you use a plastic tubing, cold weather will make it too stiff and bites will not register. Soft tubing allows for immediate movement. I rarely use them but do acknowledge that in experienced hands they can prove deadly for bream.

The quivertip has probably taken over from the swingtip, as it overcomes the above problems. Quivertips are also available in different grades of test curve, but 1oz for delicate bites in stillwaters, to 3oz which is ideal for faster rivers. The quivertip can be tightened up to the bait so that it has a slight curve in it and will therefore register drop-back bites as well as pulling round in the usual bite.

If your tips are plain white or plain black, I suggest painting them black and white in sections, like a zebra crossing. That allows for either bright shiny glares on the surface or dark backgrounds of rushes and weeds. In low light, you can end up with 'twitcher's eye', when you stare at the tip so long that you think it's moving. This is when you should use a target board, a twelve-inch square white board with a fan of black lines drawn across it. The tips, either quivertip or swingtip, are tensioned up about 4in from the board, allowing you to see the slightest movement against the painted lines. The board also stops the sensitive tips from swaying around in the wind. They should be positioned as low over the water as possible. Should you get a slack-line bite, tighten up the line by turning the reel handle slowly until the indicator is back in the original position, but stay sharp as the fish may have bumped the lead or feeder at the other end and may drag the tip round sharply as you retighten!

Bobbins

I use bobbin indicators when I have a big bait like a bunch of lobworms or several grains of sweetcorn tipped with maggots. The amount of movement of either swingtips or quivertips before I strike simply isn't enough to let the bream get the bigger bait in his mouth. I want it to move at least a foot or so before I strike, so I use either a running leger or a running paternoster cast out, and set the rods in rests with the tips pointing straight at the baits. The bobbins tension 2ft of slack between the butt and the first ring, so the bream has plenty of free space to take the bait properly. There are indicator supports available called monkey climbers but I don't like them as there is always some friction to a taking fish. Use either a small coil of silver paper, a shop-bought plastic bobbin or a circle of plastic spine from a book binding. My reel bale arm is closed and I strike as soon as the bobbin is about to touch the rod ring.

I was fishing Ballinamore one evening with Nigel Newport and Jerry Airey. Jerry isn't known for his excessive catches with swingtip or quiver-

For fishing bobbins as indicators you need to support the rods in rests, pointing them straight where you have cast to minimise friction on the rod rings. Hit bream bites very early, before the bobbin has risen to the butt ring.

tip and stubbornly stuck to bobbins coupled to optonic bite alarms. Both Nigel and I were fishing on the quivertip and thought Jerry's approach was hilarious. However I have to admit that in the nearly twenty years I have known Jerry, that was the first time he ever outfished us. He landed eight bream to Nigel's two and my one!

Floats

A selection of four different wagglers from long-bodied to thin unbodied. Get a couple of each and replace them as you lose them. Get three or four bodied Avons taking heavier shot, and three different weights of stick floats. That's all you need for floatfishing. I would suggest getting just one slider float, because you can always use the larger wagglers as sliders.

Swimfeeders

Take a range of feeders from block-ends to Drennans, wire-frames to plastic open-ended. You need some different weights to fish with them, and of course you should get a range of non-toxic weights for leger fishing. I suggest you get a couple of dozen small Berkley barrel swivels and link swivels for tying up either running legers or paternosters, and for making extensions to your feeder links. Buy a couple of packets of the small leger stops and go to your local model shop for the small-diameter silicon tube as a shock absorber for feeder and leads.

Baits

There can't be much that the bream doesn't feed on at some time or other, but there are some that definitely work better than most.

Sweetcorn

This is a very much underrated bait for bream. Most club waters ban tins and you therefore need to empty the contents into a container. Sometimes this isn't practical, especially when you open up several tins, put them into a bucket and arrive at the swim to find someone else there. I now buy my corn in 3-lb freezer packs, take it to the water in frozen form, and what I don't use I pop back into the cool box I take with me. I can then refreeze it when I get back home. Sweetcorn can go off very quickly in hot weather and I cannot afford to keep wasting it by opening tins and then not using it. Besides, a 3-lb freezer pack is a far cheaper way of buying it, and you can break it down into 8-oz bags for single sessions when you get home. A single grain of sweetcorn tipped off with either a couple of maggots or a brandling is a great bait, especially for river bream. It makes a good particle saturation bait over a bed of groundbait, but beware—you can't put enough corn in an Irish swim if a big shoal moves in. They eat it as fast as you throw it in.

Bread

It sounds too basic to be true, but the simple fact is breadflake is one of the best, yet underused, baits of modern times. Large baits on a size 10 or 8 hook, dipped in a sweet flavouring and cast out, is good for bigger specimens, but even a three-pounder will take this bait. Fish on a pater-

An underrated bait for bream is sweetcorn. The author used just one tin to take this 118lb 7oz haul of bream and tench from Hollybush pit 5 on the opening day of the season. The swim was not prebaited.

noster with a support boom to keep it over soft bottom weed and you will hit tench and carp as well as the bream. There are plenty of flavourings available in tackle shops and I advise using the sweeter ones for bream.

Worms

These are probably the best bait for bream. I've baited swims heavily with groundbait laced with bottles of worm extract, but it doesn't get the same response as a groundbait mix full of chopped up live worms. I would say that the majority of my 100-lb bags have come either directly to worm baits or to cocktail baits where worm is on the hook. Two cocktail baits spring immediately to mind. Sweetcorn (a single grain) when tipped off with a small redworm is good, as is a lobworm tipped with a couple of white maggots. I like to fish the former in conjunction with a swimfeeder, but the larger lobworm takes the bigger fish when fished on a leger rig. I also occasionally snap the tail off a larger worm when fishing in a slow- or fast-moving river to let the juices trickle out. I'm always amazed at how good worms are when I think that the number of times a bream comes across them in the natural state must be limited. Apart from a newly flooded water, where worms come out of the bed of grass in their thousands, they must hardly ever find them. It must be the smell and you can get more smell in the water by snapping the tail off. Chub anglers know the value of fishing with a lob tail anyway, but I never waste anything. I chuck it in the groundbait mix!

The author admires a big Yately bream. This particular shoal take advantage of the feed put in by carp anglers and tend to respond to particle baits.

Baits

I tip the big worm with two white maggots in clear-water, daytime fishing, when the white maggots stand out as a 'target' to attract the fish to the worm. I also believe that the small fish attack the maggots and their

If the water you intend fishing is hard fished by both match anglers and pleasure fishermen, use a bait tray to give you instant access to a choice of hookbaits.

One of the best mixes for holding a shoal of bream in the swim—brown crumb, a little bran and some casters—produced another 'ton-up' haul for the author.

activity is picked up by the bream so that they move in to see what's happening. Once they get close enough to see the maggots they pick up the smell of the worm.

Maggots

I am a great believer in white maggots, not yellow, pink, blue, bronze or green. If you put enough whites in the fish will eat them. Having said that I would urge you to try double or single red maggots. I have seen them used to good effect as a change bait from whites so often that it must be worth trying. I cannot think why this should be so, but Norman Wilkinson, an angler I was on a promotion with a few years ago, used them all the time. Just before I arrived with Nigel Newport for a session, he called to say that he had just taken his first 'ton' ever from the Shannon. They were caught almost exclusively on double reds. His theory was that the bream thought they were giant bloodworm, which they feed on heavily in the late spring and early summer as the water warms and the bloodworm become more active. It's as good a theory as I've heard, but I have never been pestered by mosquitoes very much in Ireland, so I wonder how much bloodworm larvae there are there. The water is very peaty, with some acidity, and I would have thought that this would affect the reproduction of the bloodworm/mosquito. Since red maggots do work, why not produce your own gozzers (large maggots with soft skin) from a piece of liver covered with damp bread and put dye into the feed to colour them? Then use a loose feed of pinkies or shop-bought red maggots with the giant red gozzers as hookbait.

When pre-baiting I put in any type of maggot, from sweepings to stretched maggots, skins—all the rubbish I can get hold of. Anglers, especially matchmen, have a fetish about using absolutely prime bait, but in my experience an initial pre-bait can be done with anything to draw fish into the area. Only on the day of fishing do I put in better bait, and certainly a good hookbait is important. Why waste good money on top bait for pre-baiting sessions when you aren't even sure whether the fish are going to be there? In hot weather you may find it useful to keep your bait container in a cool box with a blue freezer block thrown in to chill it down. Sweating maggots soon expire and are then only good for pre-baiting.

Casters

These are among the best baits for bigger bream—say over 4lb. Small fry are notorious for attacking maggots and 'skinning' them, but they have trouble biting into the shell of a caster. Bigger fish can pop them easily and once they get a taste for the juices inside they usually feed very heavily. Casters are expensive to buy because of the labour-intensive operation of running them off as they turn to casters, riddling them, separating them and chilling them. The best colour is light brown, and the darker the shell the more likely it is to be a floater. At this stage they are useless as hookbait or feed, except in a mix of groundbait. If you buy a couple of pints and fish on a hot day they will turn darker in a few hours. They should be kept cool so try a blue freezer block in a cool box. Some anglers make a special polystyrene liner with a blue block tucked into the side.

A good way to test casters is to put them in a large bait container of water. Skim off those that have turned to floaters and retain the rest for loose feed and hookbait. When you mix floaters in with groundbait make sure you squash them, otherwise they will float up to the surface. After a session, if you have maggots left over, let them start to turn to casters (they stop moving and start to tighten), then put them in the fridge when you get home. That way you save money on buying from the tackle shop again.

I used to get the leftovers—2 gallons at a time—from a tackle dealer in Hawley many years ago, who thought floaters were good for nothing. I would mash the lot up with a piece of wood, then use a light groundbait to bind the juices. It was much like treading grapes, but much more repulsive! I took some pretty good bags on those mashed floaters, so try to find a use for everything.

Remember that if you use a single caster on a light float rig for smaller bream you need a special caster hook. These are very fine, designed to penetrate the outer shell without splitting it open. Every time you get a bite, wind in to check whether the shell has been popped. With maggots

An angler with an Irish bream. You need a lot of groundbait to hold a big shoal of these fish, a fact which many anglers underestimate, and therefore fail to catch continuously.

you can make a short strike with your wrist, only move the float a few feet, and if you don't connect leave it there for another bite. With casters, one bite means either a hooked fish or a shelled caster.

Boilies

These modern baits now come pre-packed, all rolled to size and ready to use. They cost money of course, and are aimed primarily at the carp angler. The idea of the boilie is to stop unwanted species whittling away at a softer paste bait when you are putting in long sessions for carp. A large bait is generally used for the carp, and by boiling the rolled baits, the anglers could put a skin on the outside to stop unwanted species leaving them with just a bare hook on a long night session. However, so many boilies are being baited in mixed fisheries now that all the other species are being attracted as well. The only way round this problem is for the carp fisherman to use a really big bait. The current baiting fashion is to lay down a particle saturation of mini-boilies as the main carpet of bait, with larger single boilies fished over the top. It's intended to get the carp interested in the huge number of mini-boilies and so lose all caution when they find the larger bait.

That sounds fine, but even though the mini-boilies are also skinned, they are just the right size to be taken by everything from bream to tench. Carp anglers don't realise how much bait they are wasting when they fire out mini-boilies. Bream are becoming interested in mini-boilies, so it's logical to use them. Fish a single or double mini-boilie on a standard running leger rig in one of the known carp swims. With all the baiting done by carp anglers, the bream shoal shouldn't be far away.

Other Baits

There are some baits which are hardly mainstream bream baits, but which I have taken bream on, sometimes in numbers. A soft pliable cheese like Edam or mild English cheddar pinched on a light hooklink, say 3lb, a size 10 hook and link leger rig picks up the odd fish, and is especially good on the Hampshire Avon and Dorset Stour, which are showing some reasonable bream catches now. Fished in tiny cubes on the same hook and rig, luncheon meat bait fishes well in stillwaters as well as rivers when anchored over a bed of sweetcorn. Tares are better used with floatfishing, and with a loose feed of hempseed. Make sure you cook both well, and use them sparingly, especially the hempseed. A light cloudbait might help.

Go Fishing for Bream

Groundbait balls can be both coloured and flavoured to suit the bream's taste. Most tackle shops offer an extensive choice of both flavours and colours.

Groundbaits

When bream fishing, remember that you can never have too much ground-bait. One of the big problems with anglers, especially those visiting Ireland for the first time, is that they don't appreciate how quickly a big shoal of bream can mop up a swim. You need to establish that they are there in the first place before the 'big fill-in', and you can do this by making a cast with your intended hookbait for ten minutes. If you don't get a line bite or a fish bite, then go easy on the groundbait. If you're sure they are in front of you, go for it in a big way.

It was Paul Harris who first introduced me to serious groundbaiting for bream. 'Irish bream are only loyal to them that feeds them' was his motto. Many northern anglers, used to putting 2lb of feed in a canal swim in a day, are stunned when you walk up with a half-hundredweight sack, throwing stick and catapult. But in Ireland there is less angling pressure and you've got to stop a big patrolling shoal dead in its tracks. They wouldn't pause in mid-fin for 2lb of feed.

On Lough Garadice in Ballinamore, for instance, they took a sounder reading from a shoal of bream half a mile long! It's impossible to overfeed that amount, so do go prepared. If you are flying over, you are obviously going to be restricted on weight. If you are driving over, the leaf springs are your limit. I've gone over with Nigel Newport taking so much groundbait that the car's steering has gone light and funny. We've put in some large amounts of feed, but then we've had some large bags of fish.

I recently read in the angling press of a 3000-lb haul of bream. It seems incredible but it did take six anglers a week to amass that total. It actually works out at barely 100lb per man per day. While unwrapping some rubbish in the attic the other day I became engrossed in some paper, faded with age and curled up. It was an old 1974 edition of the *Angling Times,* and on the front page was a report of a Lancashire angler landing 400lb of bream between 4 and 7lb in just nine hours! Now that's what I call bream fishing. (It was on worm from the Shannon as a point of interest.)

Just as I like plain white maggots, so I like plain white groundbait. In Ireland you can buy pig meal, which is a cheap and easy way to bait up. In fact that 400-lb catch was baited with pig meal. Or you can get maize meal. This is a yellowish grain, and when it is mixed with water it gains the consistency of superglue. We got stuck up so badly on one session that the groundbait ball wouldn't come out of the throwing stick! This material is best mixed with bran, or layer's mash as some call it, mixing it together 50:50 when dry. The minute you add water to maize meal it becomes sticky. I only use it for pre-baiting, as I much prefer the better break-up qualities of 'proper' groundbait.

Mix together coarse white crumb, a little brown and a handful or two of bran per bucket. Buy them all in sacks, as it saves money. Although this makes a good feed for bream, consistency in the mix is also important. You don't want to be spraying it around willy nilly. Accurate throwing, with perhaps the bonus of a swim marker, ensures that your hookbait lies over the baited area. You want the ball of feed to stay together in the air but break up on impact with the water. In rivers, mix it harder by reducing the bran and brown groundbait so that it binds together better. I like mine as sloppy as possible, yet able to bind together when I squeeze it hard.

The Continental matchmen must take the credit for popularising additives in groundbaits. The French for instance concentrate on peanut, hempseed, bread and maize for the small fish. Taking advantage of the amazing range of flavourings now available in tackle shops, you could do a lot worse than molasses or vanilla, both of which are sweet. Bream have a very definite sweet tooth. Also try Scopex or chocolate malt, both of which are the 'secret' bream additives of the moment. Recently, Nigel Newport had a good winter haul from the Yateley complex of pits by using Marcel Vandeneynde Bream Additive in his groundbait mix, with crushed hempseed. I have a preference for vanilla extract. The sure way to get these concentrates mixed in evenly is to put a capful into the bucket of water you are going to dampen the dry mix with. If you add it to the dry mix, it soaks into the first area it reaches and doesn't spread thoroughly.

As for the distribution of the mix, much depends on how many maggots you put in the feed. If you put in a lot the wriggling maggots will break up the balls fast, so there's no point in squeezing them together and lining them up ready for a major launch—by the time you reach for the fourth ball it will have broken apart. It is better to use a few maggots, or better still crushed casters. Then you can line the balls up, with one man mixing and the other firing them out. The best session I ever had was with Nigel Newport and the late Denis Breen, the fishing policeman of Ballinamore. We were trying to stop a legendary half-mile Garadice bream shoal. Denis arrived on Connolly shore with his panda car, fully uniformed, rolled up his sleeves and started to work the mix. Naturally enough we both joined in and three sacks of groundbait later had the most incredible pyramid of balls stacked up like baked bean cans in a supermarket.

Denis had had the forethought to bring the awesome Ballinamore throwing stick. It was 6ft long, made of copper tubing with a Fray Bentos pie tin bolted on as the cup. I firmed up each ball and passed it to Nigel who dropped it in the cup to a shout of 'Pull!' Denis let fly, standing back to the water and belting them forty yards over his head. Of course things got out of hand (don't they always?), and it developed into a race to see how high, how far, and how many Denis could get in the air at one time. The records were 80ft, 70 yards and three respectively. By the time the pile had gone Denis was sweating in his uniform and the panda car was caked with groundbait. We were all soaking wet. The following dawn we popped out over 110lb of bream and pike and saw so many bream rolling on the surface that I can well believe the half-mile sonar reading. 'They look sick or stunned,' said Nigel. I wasn't surprised, from the amount of feed that went in!

Bream fishing is fun. You can go for the big fish or you can go for the big bags. Although I have in the past staggered miles with heaps of tackle and trollies of groundbait through boggy Irish fields, I have now had a change of heart. My advice now is: Take the minimum of tackle, two or three keepnets in case you feel you are going to 'bag up', but plenty of bait. The advantages of travelling light were brought home to me on a trip a few years back to St John's lake, Ballinamore. Nigel, Jerry and I were taken there by Denis, and the walk to the swim was not short. Jerry, as usual, had everything but the kitchen sink. The day started badly for him when he stepped out of his shoe into his wader, missed and went straight in a very fresh cowpat. Nigel marched off and I followed, and by the time Jerry arrived, staggering under his immense load, we had a couple of skimmers in the net. 'Don't fish there, its a rubbish swim, and shallow,' Denis told him. But Jerry's brain was in overdrive, and he said he would fish where he wanted. It took him half an hour to get sorted out, by which time our catches had confirmed that we weren't going to do much business today. We agreed on a move and started to pack up.

Nigel and I arrived sweating at the car—it was now 11am on a sunny day. Nigel was in hysterics, watching the bushes across the field some 400 yards away through his binoculars. He passed them to me, still giggling. 'Look at him,' he laughed. I focused and there was Jerry, eight rods, three tackle boxes, half a dozen keepnets, and his best match rod up a tree. I could see his mouth moving at double speed as he cursed and wrenched. It happened of course—the carbon snapped up the tree. We doubled over as he hurled the tackle around in a rage, screaming obscenities. We both crawled closer and hid behind some gorse waiting for him to come past. I had the camera, as I wanted a picture of Jerry, now looking like Donald Duck after completing an SAS course in the Brecon Beacons. There was a herd of cows by him as he came past and they followed him. He tried to turn and swear at them but the holdall strap was pressed against his adam's apple. A stifled squeak emerged. I snapped my picture and we legged it back to the car.

As he came up he collapsed in a heap. Nigel couldn't control his laughter. 'It's not *that* funny,' I said. 'It bloody well is,' said Nigel, 'Take a look at the bottom of his tackle box.' I opened the lid, took out some trays, and there in the bottom were five big rocks. Nigel was rolling around. 'I put them in last night. He's carried them all the way to the swim, and all the way back again!' I looked at Jerry, who obviously didn't see the funny side of this. I recall his words, as they echoed round the hillside. 'I'm not fishing with you two b_____s again!' But he did of course—such is the wonder of bream fishing.